# Knights

Written By Joanne Mattern

Illustrated By Chris Marrinan

ROURKE PUBLISHING

Vero Beach, Florida 32964

www.rourkepublishing.com

Edited by Katherine M. Thal
Illustrated by Chris Marrinan
Art Direction and Page Layout by Renee Brady


Photo Credits: © Donald Gruener: Title Page, 4, 5, 26, 27, 28, 29, 30, 31, 32; © Duncan Walker: 26; © james steidl: 27; © Alan Crawford: 28


**Library of Congress Cataloging-in-Publication Data**

Mattern, Joanne, 1963-
  Knights / Joanne Mattern.
      p. cm. -- (Warriors graphic illustrated)
  Includes bibliographical references and index.
  ISBN 978-1-60694-431-8 (alk. paper)
  ISBN 978-1-60694-540-7 (soft cover)
  1. Knights and knighthood--Juvenile literature.. 2. Civilization,
Medieval--Juvenile literature.  I. Title.
  CR4513.M385 2010
  940.1--dc22

                        2009020488


Printed in the USA

CG/CG

www.rourkepublishing.com - rourke@rourkepublishing.com
Post Office Box 643328  Vero Beach, Florida 32964

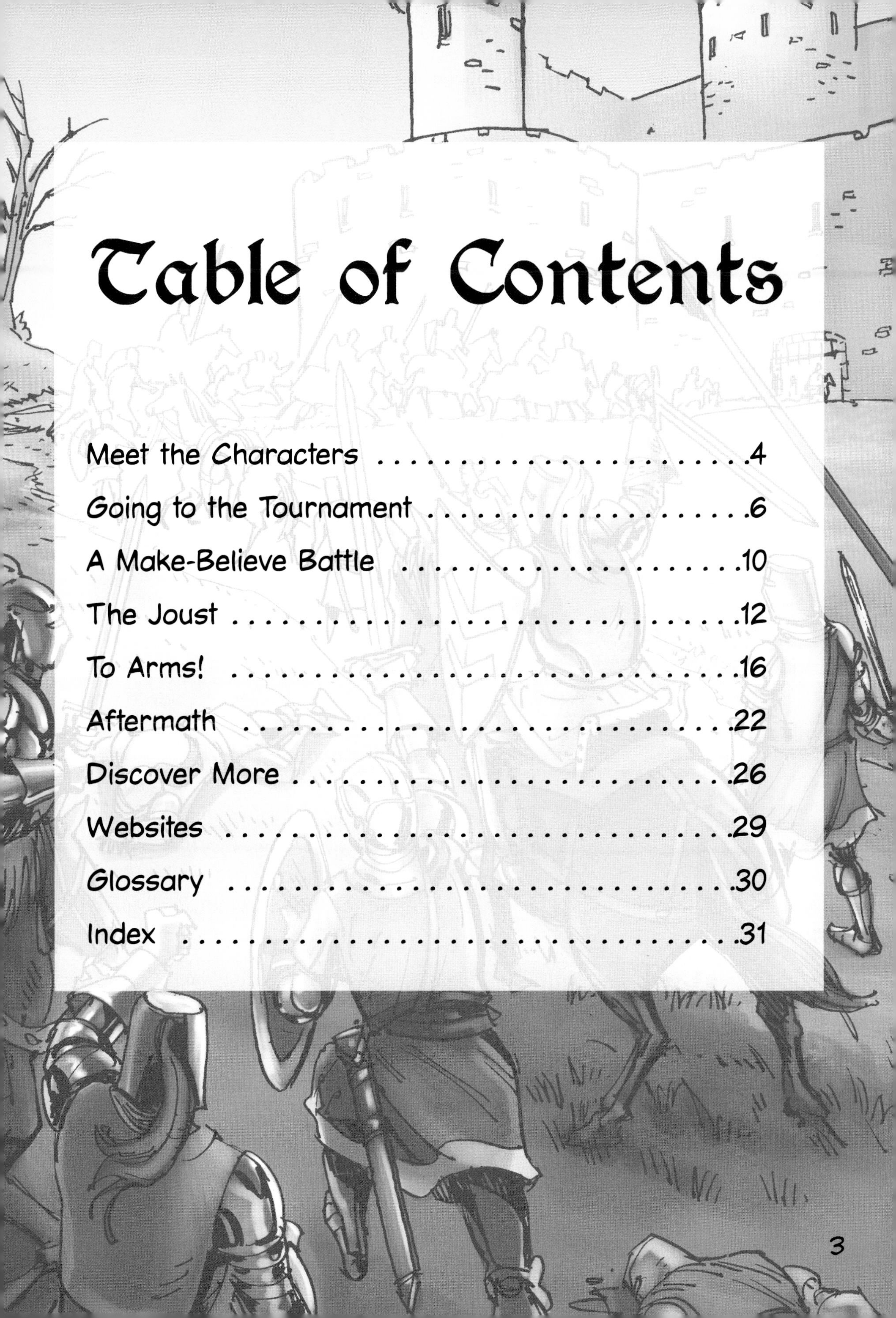

# Table of Contents

## Simon

Simon is a young man who is sparring in his first tournament as a knight. At one time, he was the squire for Lord Roger. He quickly proves his worth to Lord Roger.

## Toby

Toby, a young boy, is Simon's squire. He helps Simon get dressed in his knight's armor before battles, and he helps him during battles.

## John

John is Simon's friend, and spars with him in a mock tournament. Later, he and Simon serve under Lord Roger's command in a real battle against Lord Andrew's army.

# Lord Roger

Lord Roger, the ruler of North Ryeland, leads the blue army. He fights Sir Nicholas in a joust.

# Sir Nicholas

Sir Nicholas, the leader of the green army, fights Lord Roger in a joust. He is an older knight.

# Lord Andrew

As ruler of South Ryeland, Lord Andrew continues to battle Lord Roger over border rights.

Note: The knights in this book are fictitous, but the events surrounding them are not.

# GOING TO THE TOURNAMENT

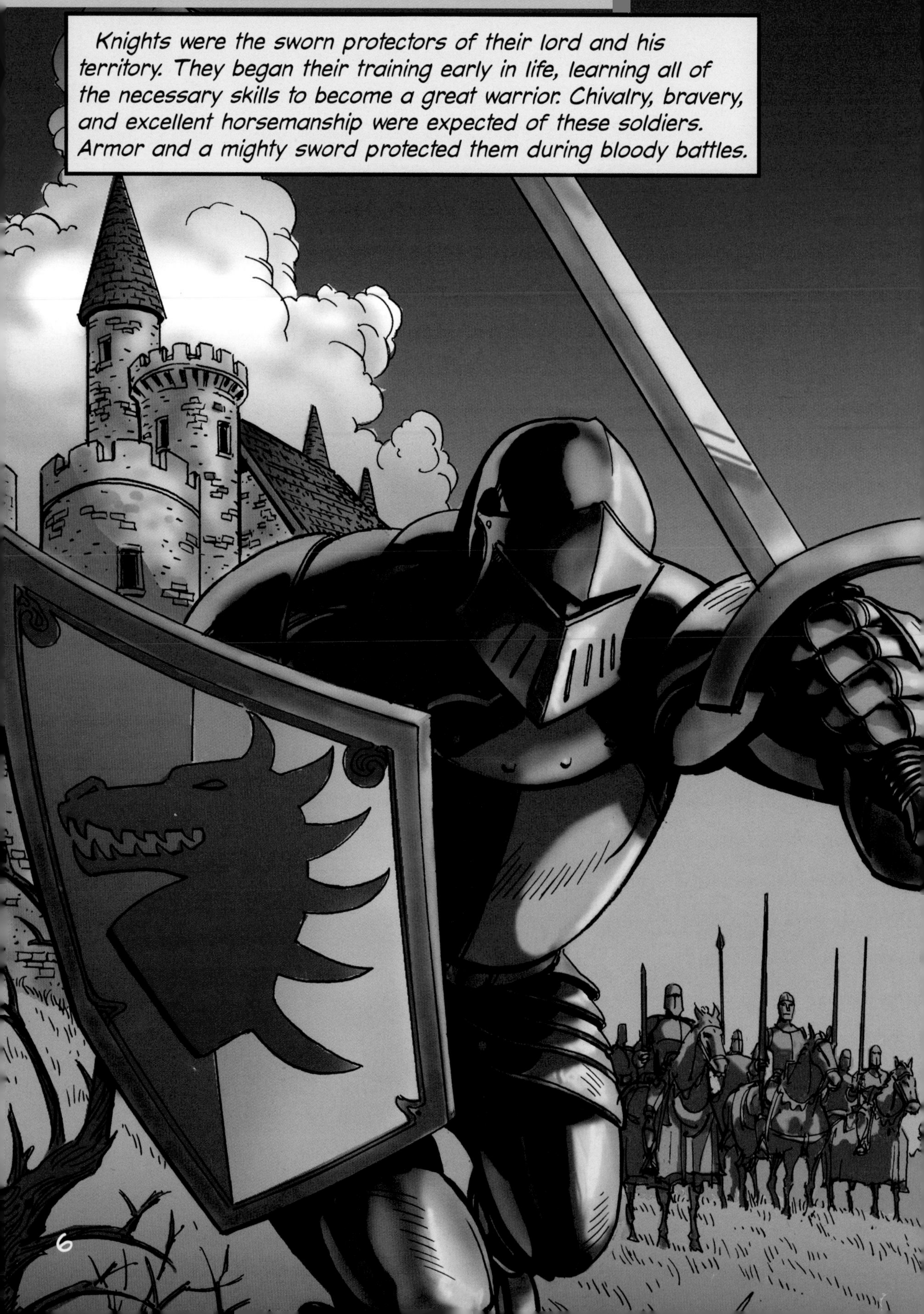
Knights were the sworn protectors of their lord and his territory. They began their training early in life, learning all of the necessary skills to become a great warrior. Chivalry, bravery, and excellent horsemanship were expected of these soldiers. Armor and a mighty sword protected them during bloody battles.

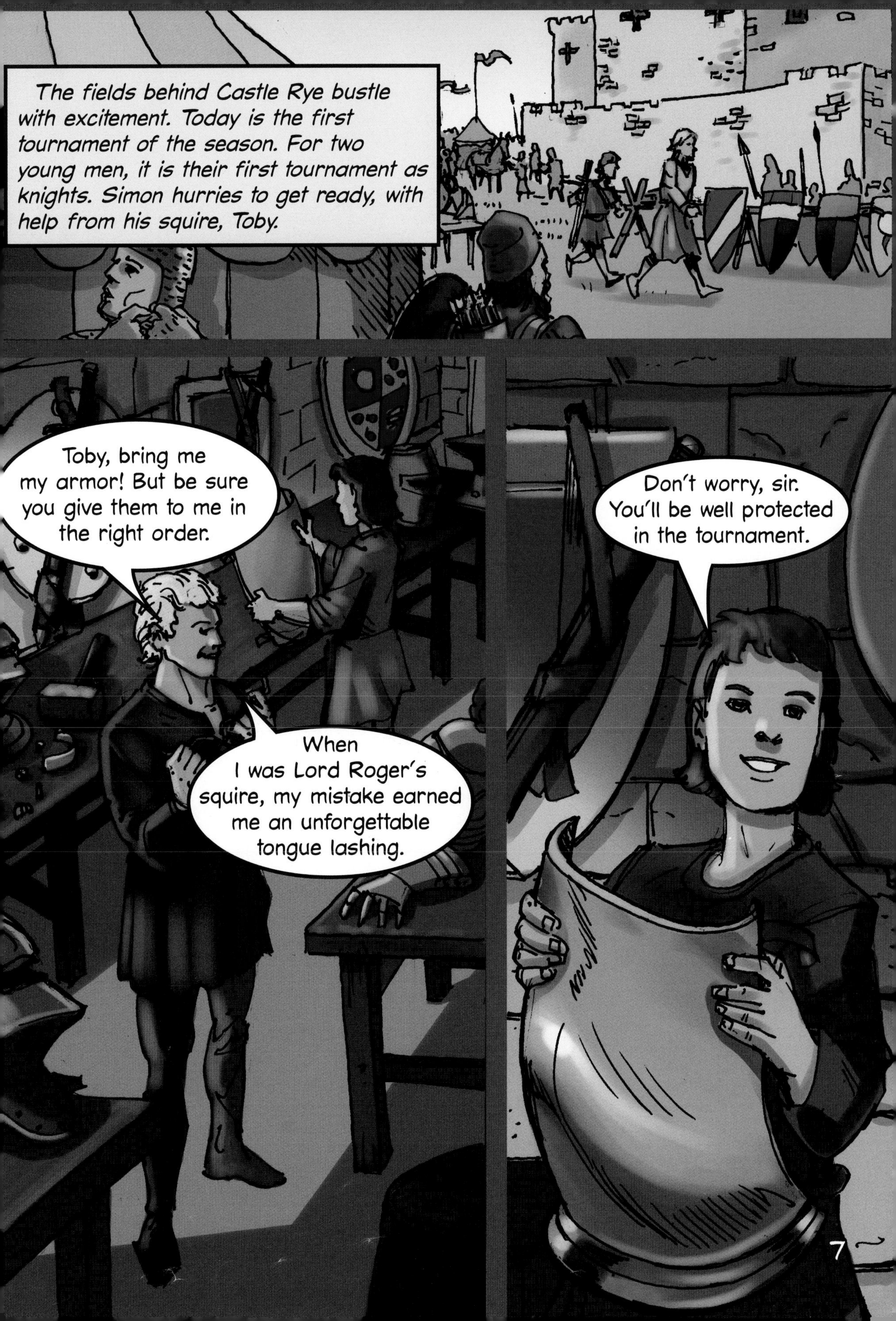
The fields behind Castle Rye bustle with excitement. Today is the first tournament of the season. For two young men, it is their first tournament as knights. Simon hurries to get ready, with help from his squire, Toby.
Toby, bring me my armor! But be sure you give them to me in the right order.
When I was Lord Roger's squire, my mistake earned me an unforgettable tongue lashing.
Don't worry, sir. You'll be well protected in the tournament.

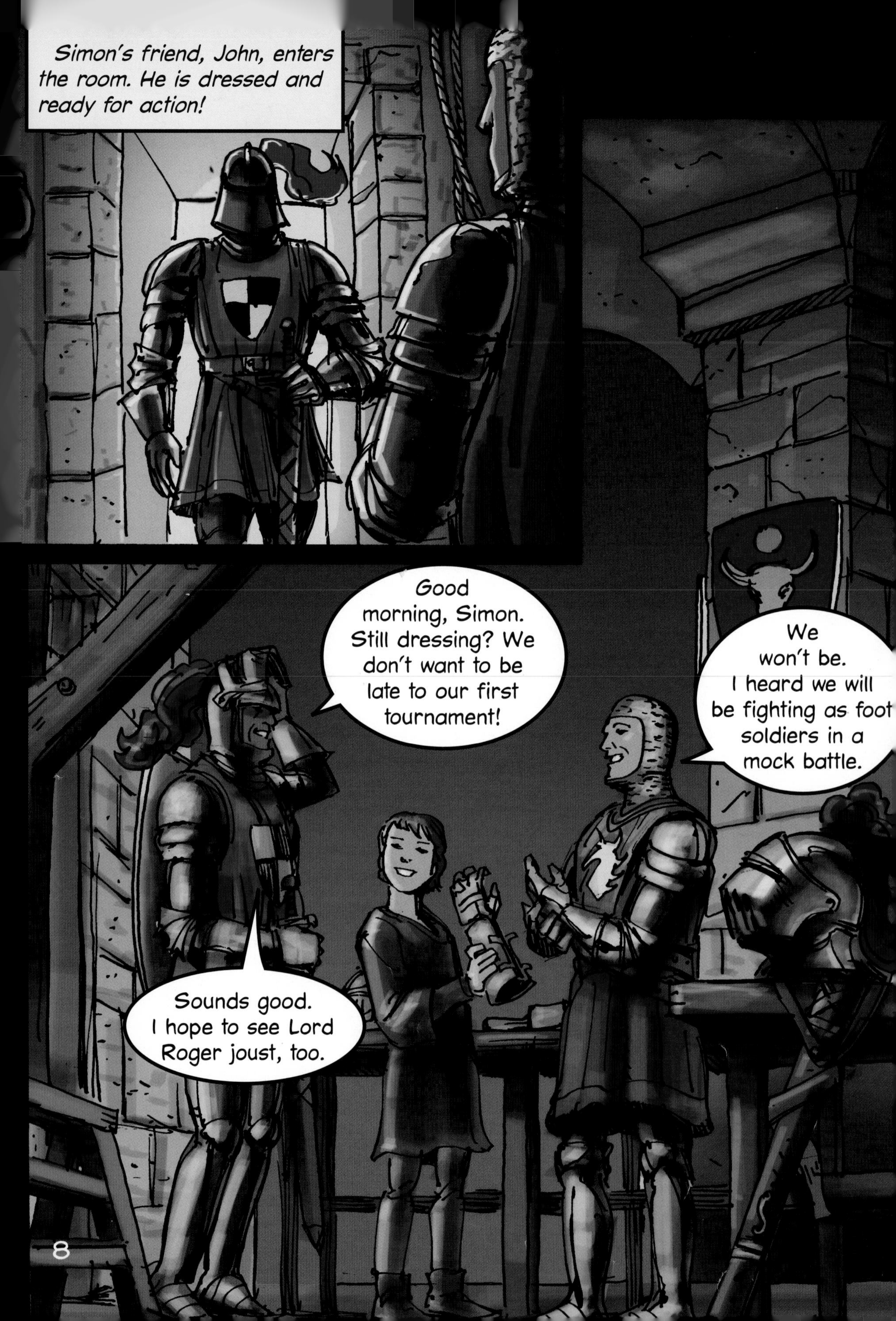
Simon's friend, John, enters the room. He is dressed and ready for action!
Good morning, Simon. Still dressing? We don't want to be late to our first tournament!
We won't be. I heard we will be fighting as foot soldiers in a mock battle.
Sounds good. I hope to see Lord Roger joust, too.

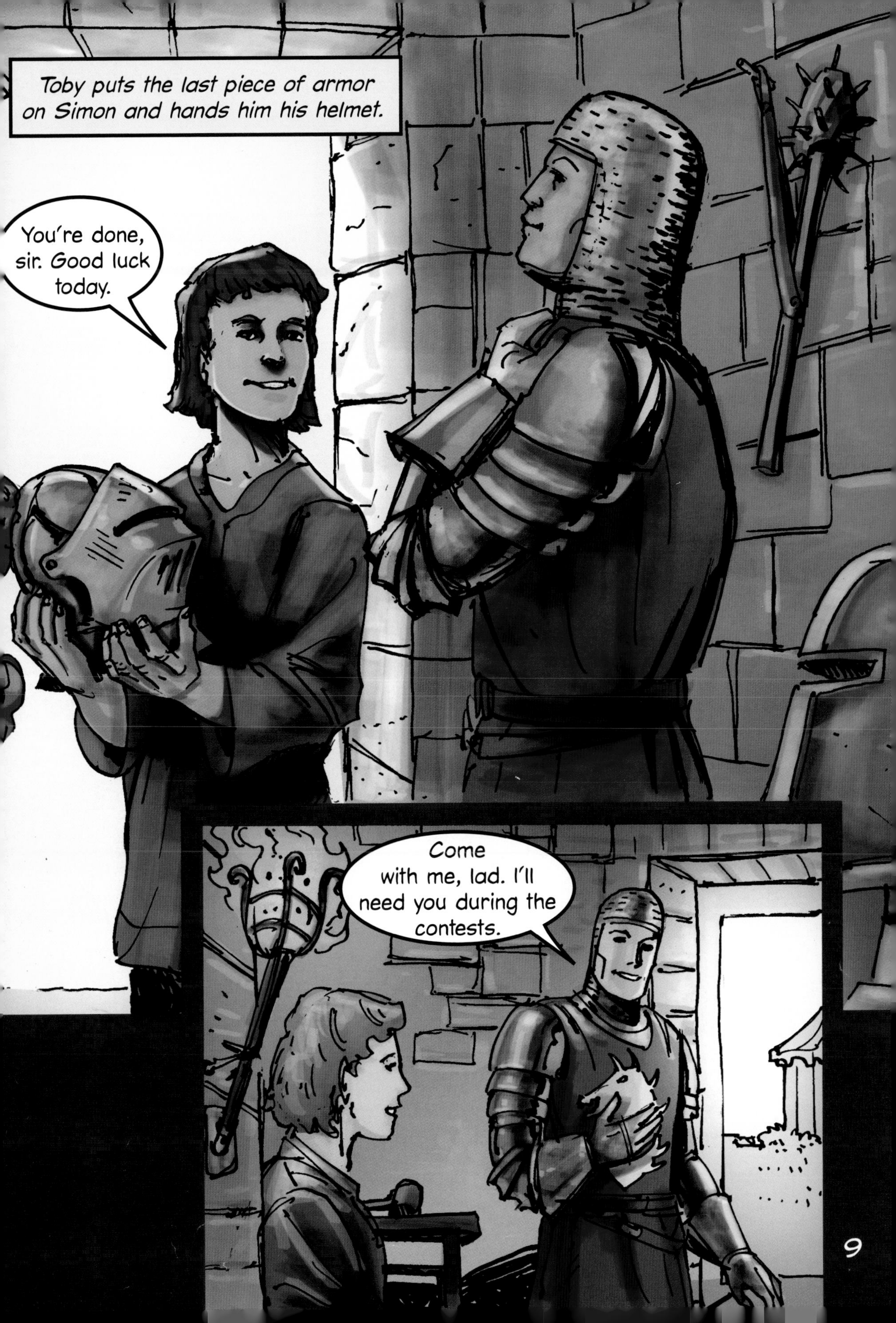
Toby puts the last piece of armor on Simon and hands him his helmet.
You're done, sir. Good luck today.
Come with me, lad. I'll need you during the contests.

# A MAKE-BELIEVE BATTLE

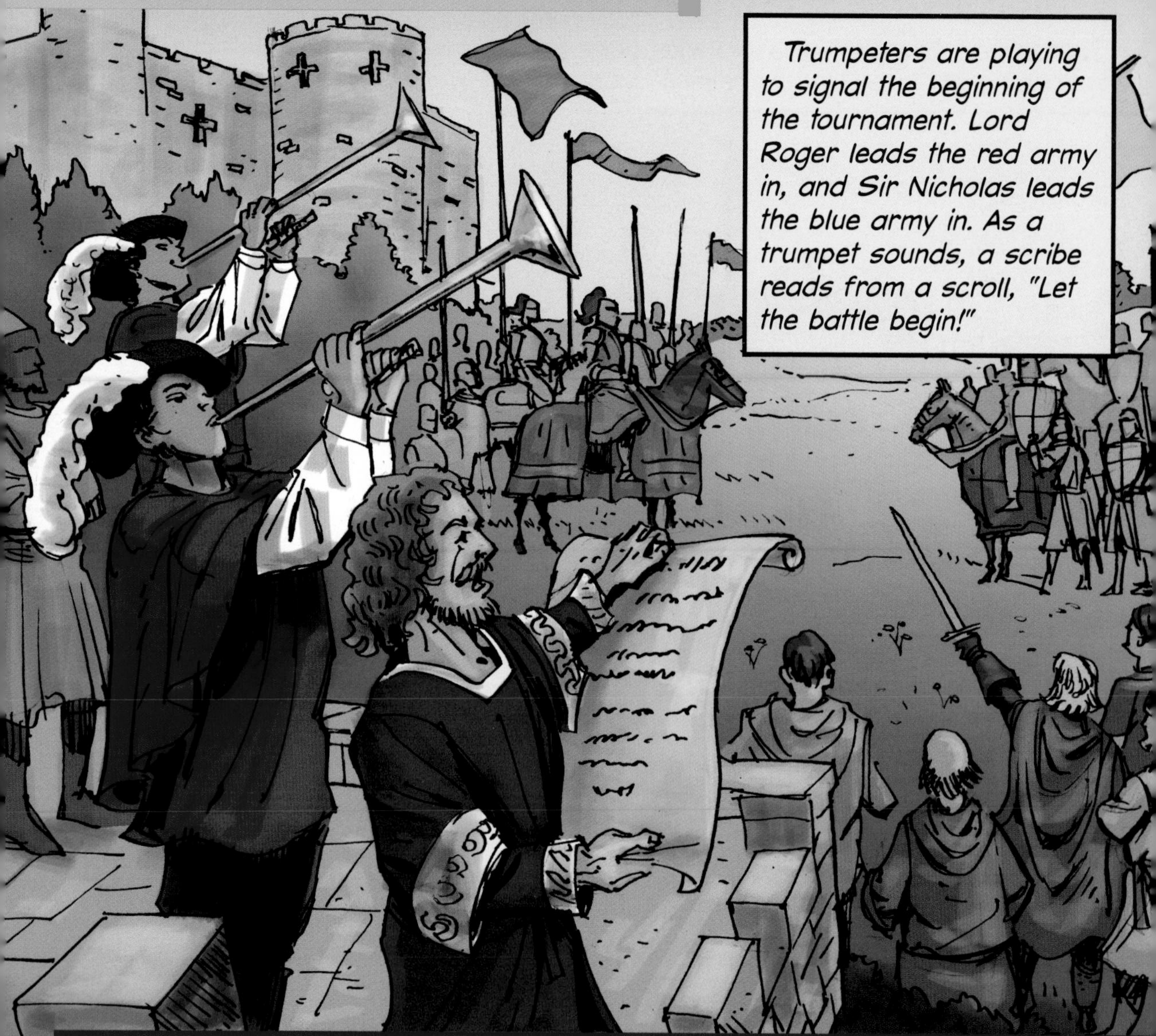

Trumpeters are playing to signal the beginning of the tournament. Lord Roger leads the red army in, and Sir Nicholas leads the blue army in. As a trumpet sounds, a scribe reads from a scroll, "Let the battle begin!"


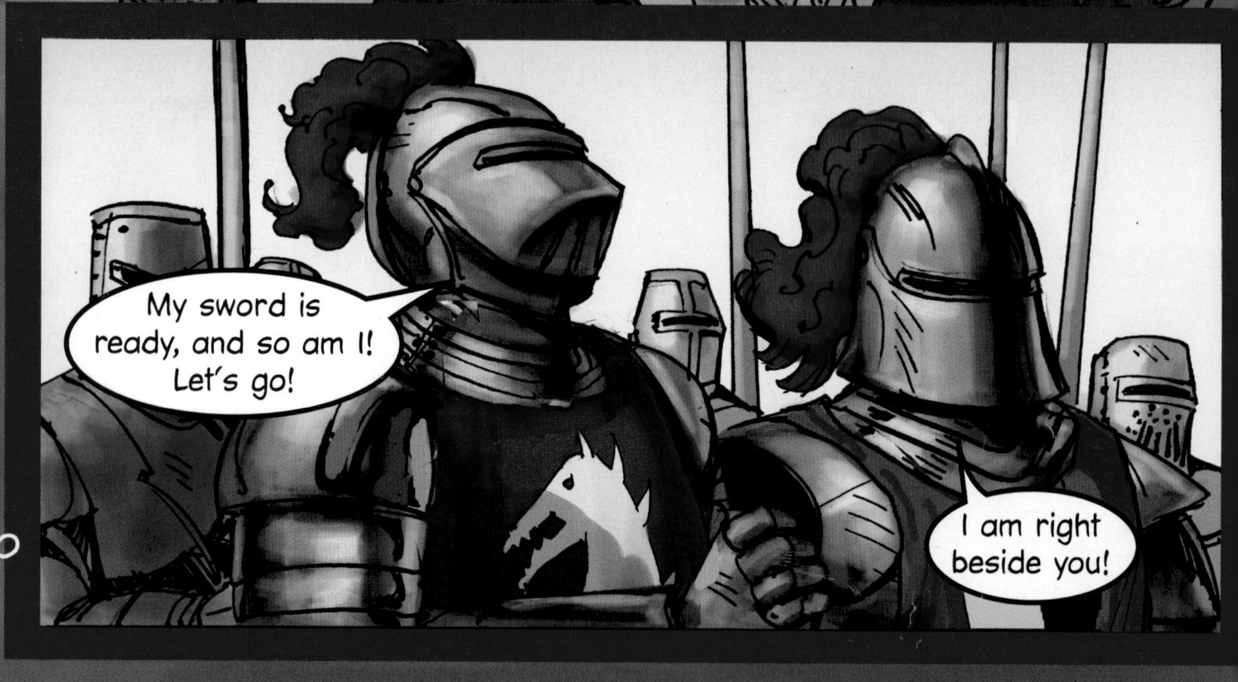

My sword is ready, and so am I! Let's go!
I am right beside you!

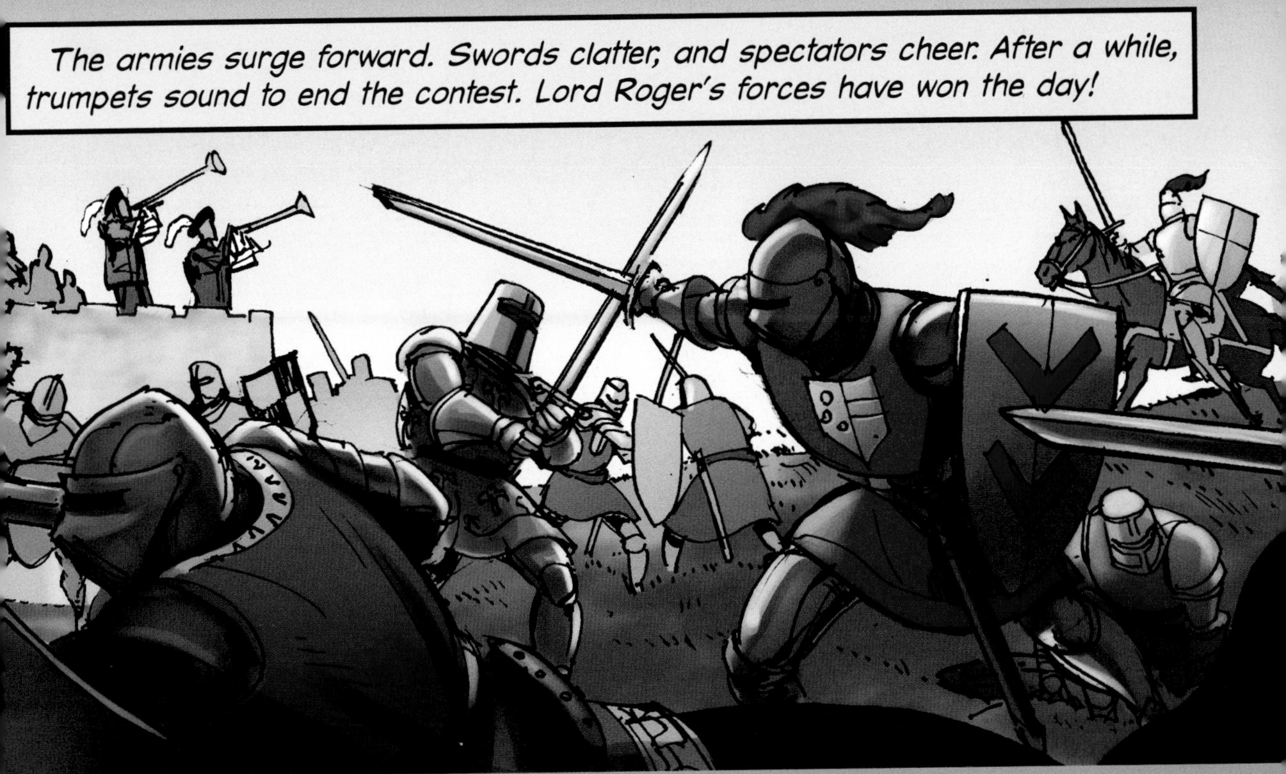
The armies surge forward. Swords clatter, and spectators cheer. After a while, trumpets sound to end the contest. Lord Roger's forces have won the day!

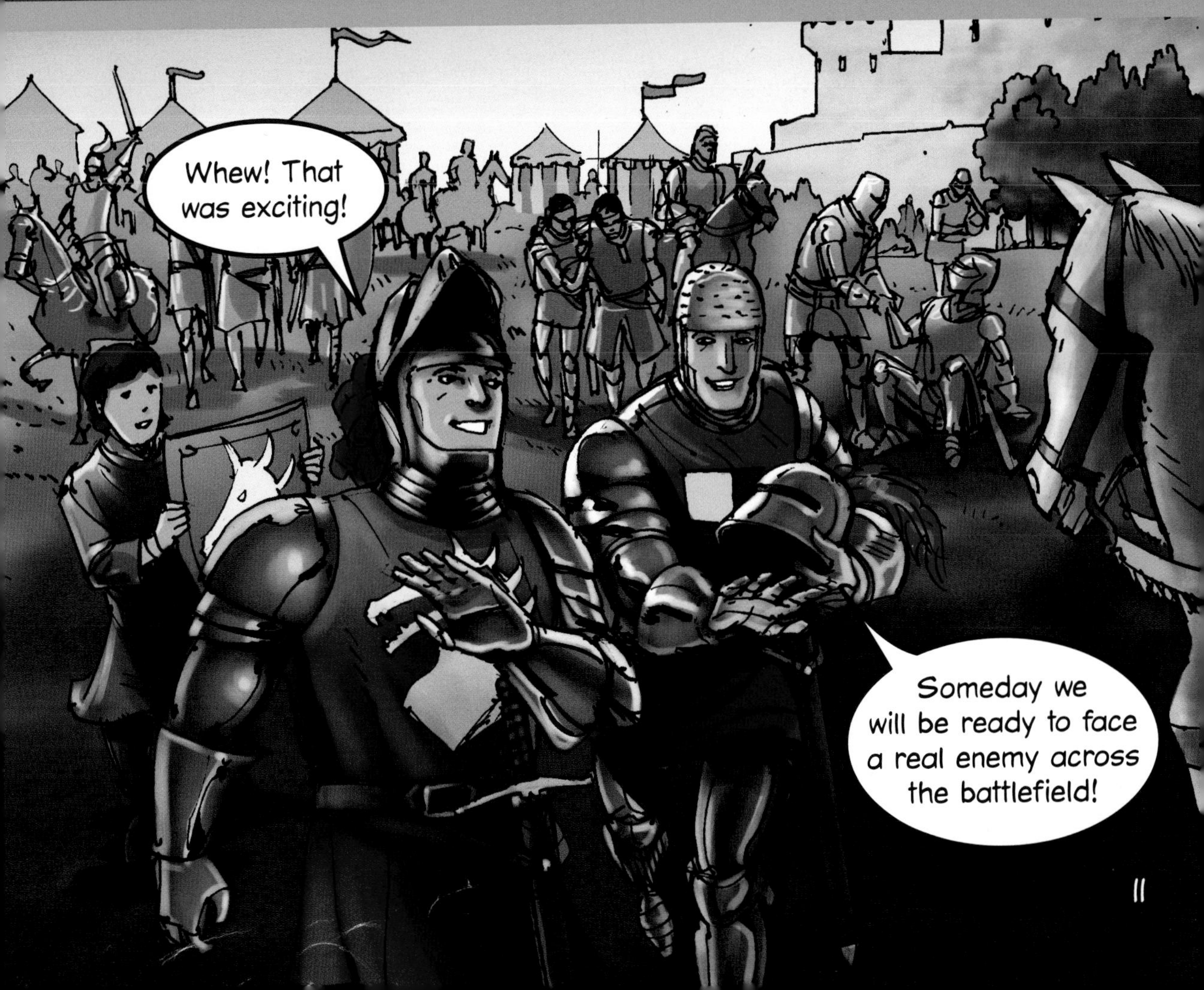
Whew! That was exciting!
Someday we will be ready to face a real enemy across the battlefield!

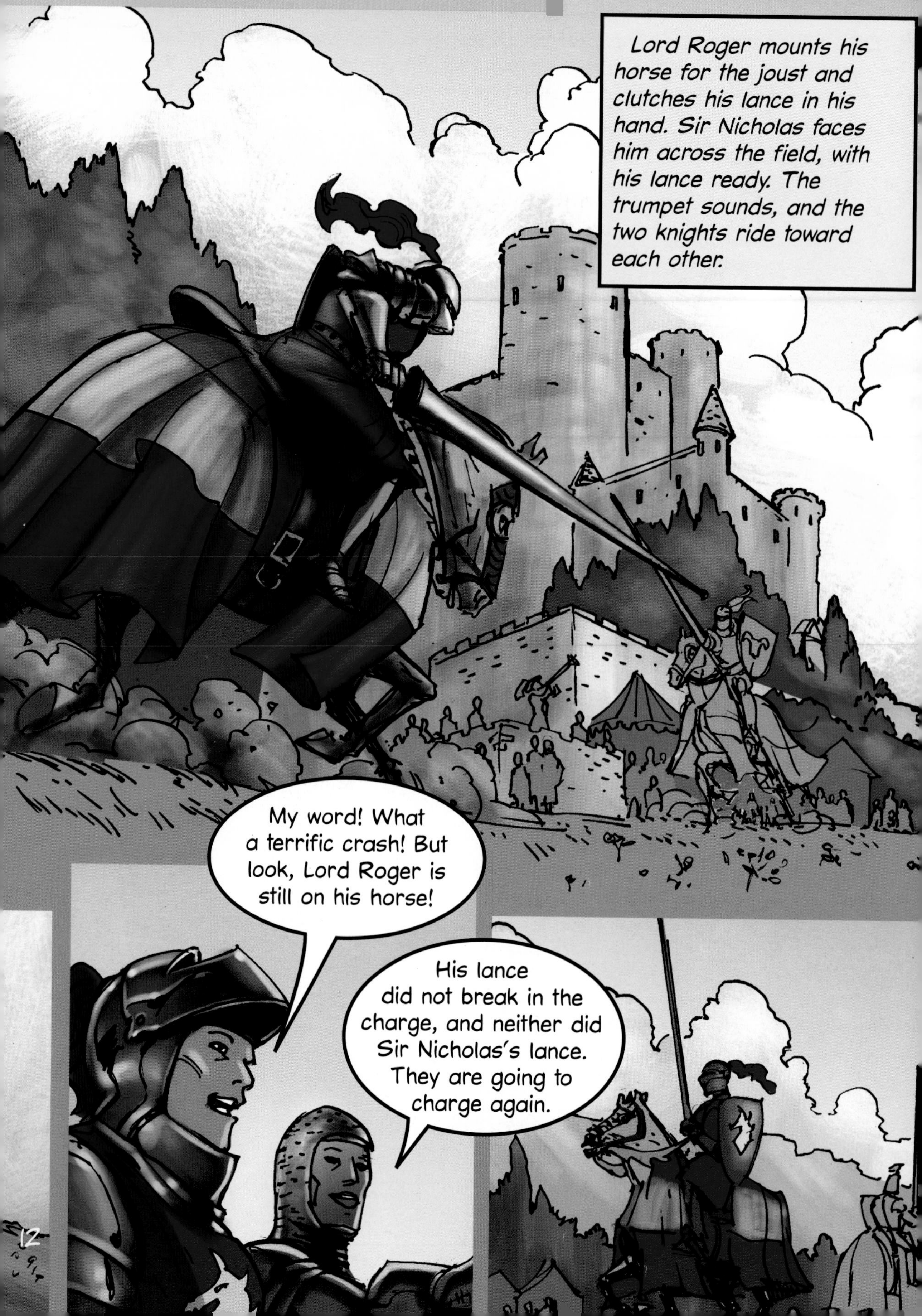
Lord Roger mounts his horse for the joust and clutches his lance in his hand. Sir Nicholas faces him across the field, with his lance ready. The trumpet sounds, and the two knights ride toward each other.
My word! What a terrific crash! But look, Lord Roger is still on his horse!
His lance did not break in the charge, and neither did Sir Nicholas's lance. They are going to charge again.

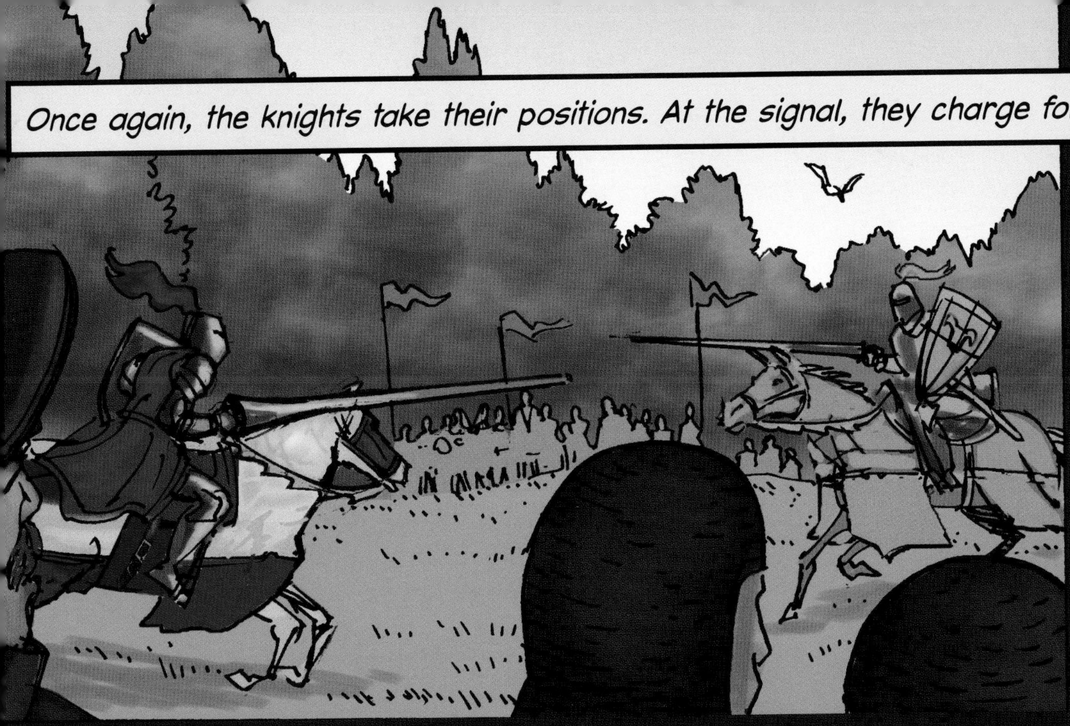
Once again, the knights take their positions. At the signal, they charge forward.

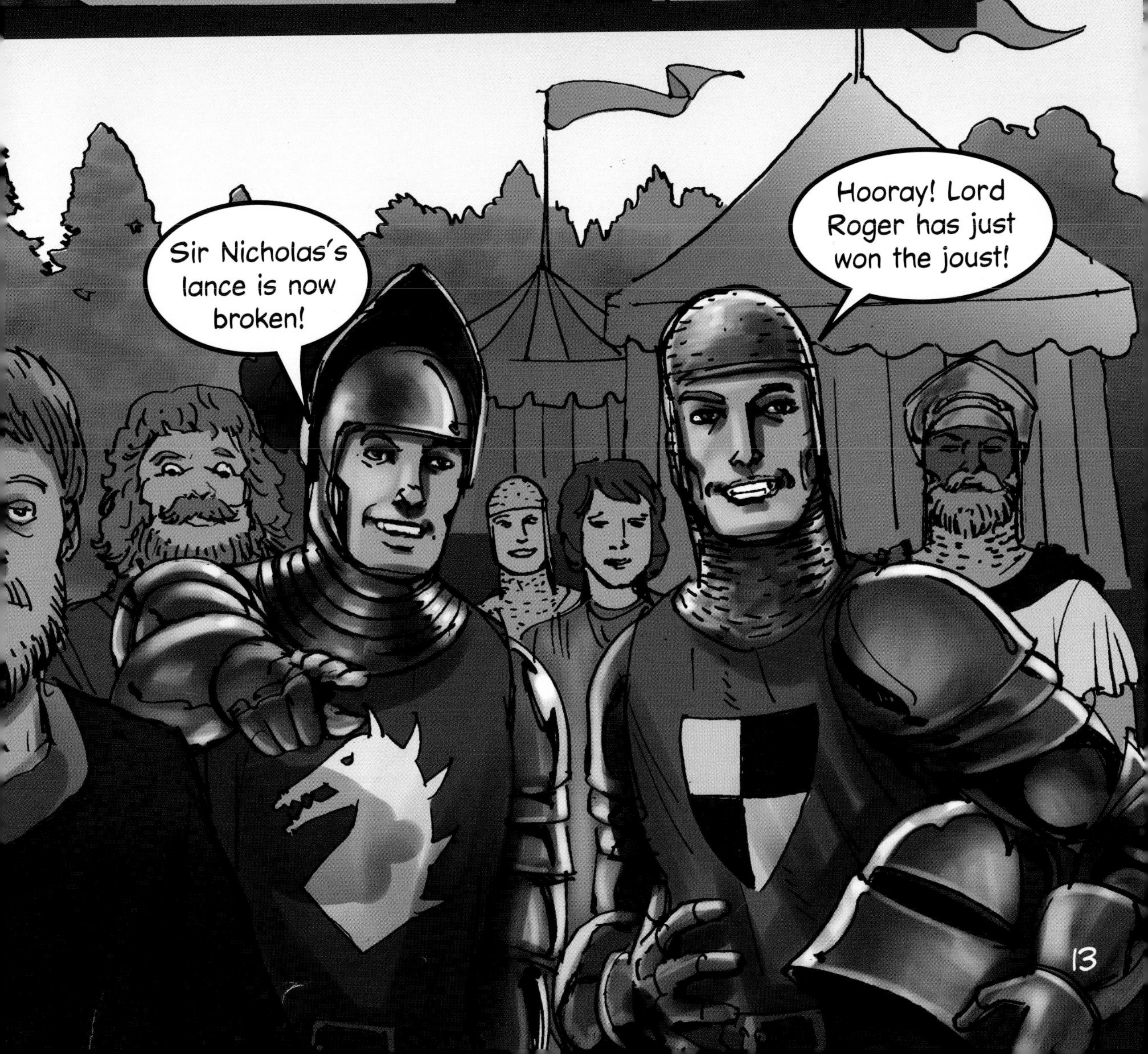
Sir Nicholas's lance is now broken!
Hooray! Lord Roger has just won the joust!

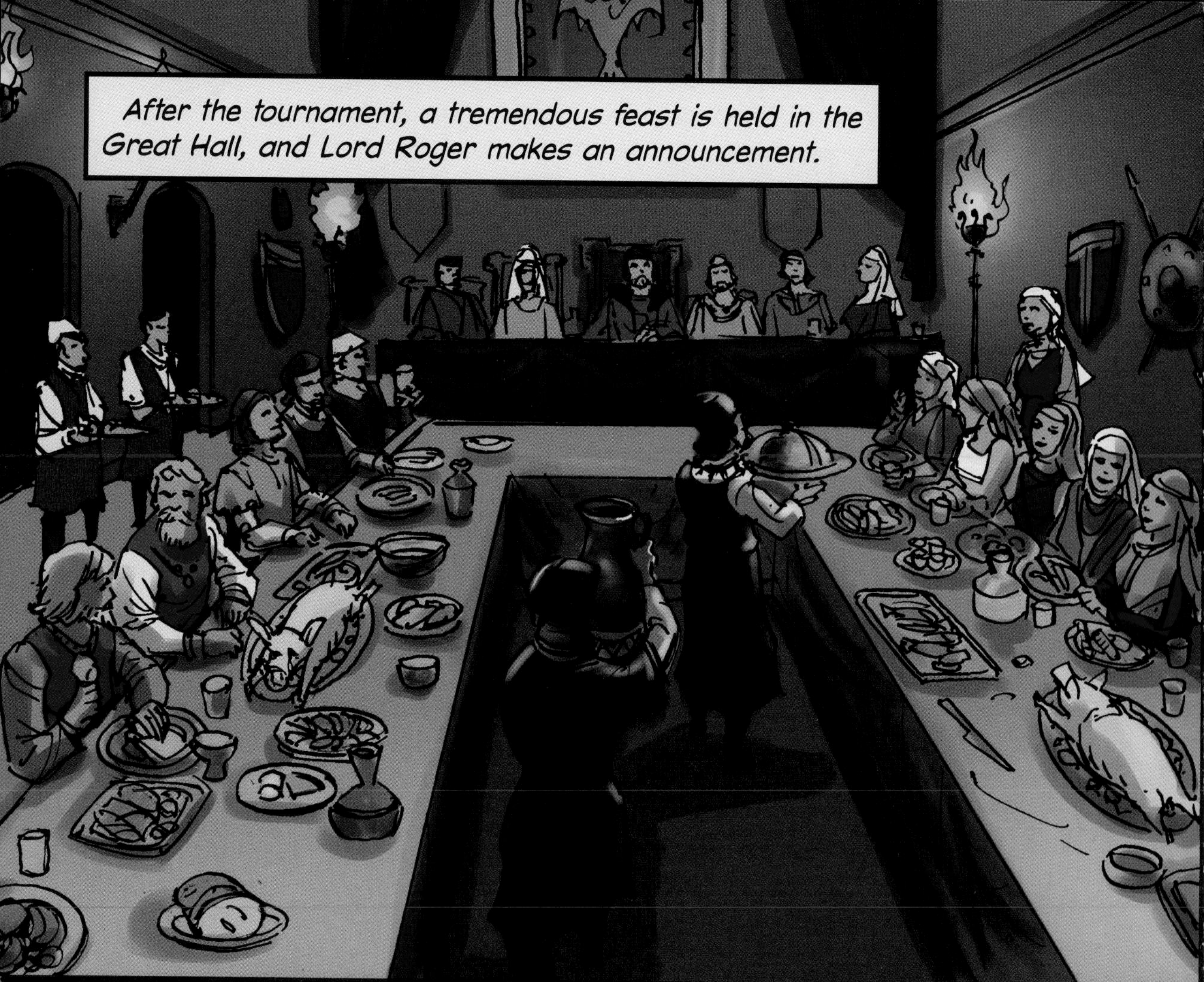
After the tournament, a tremendous feast is held in the Great Hall, and Lord Roger makes an announcement.

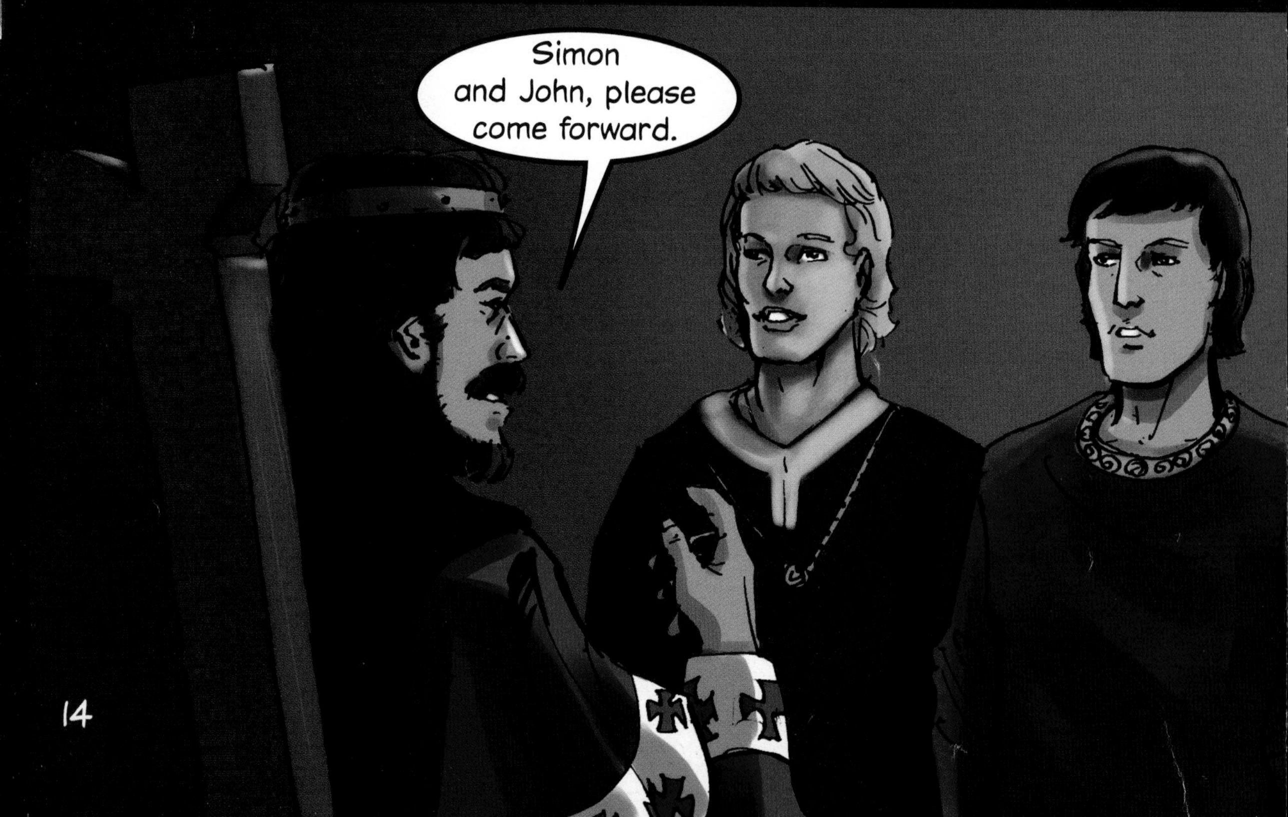
Simon and John, please come forward.

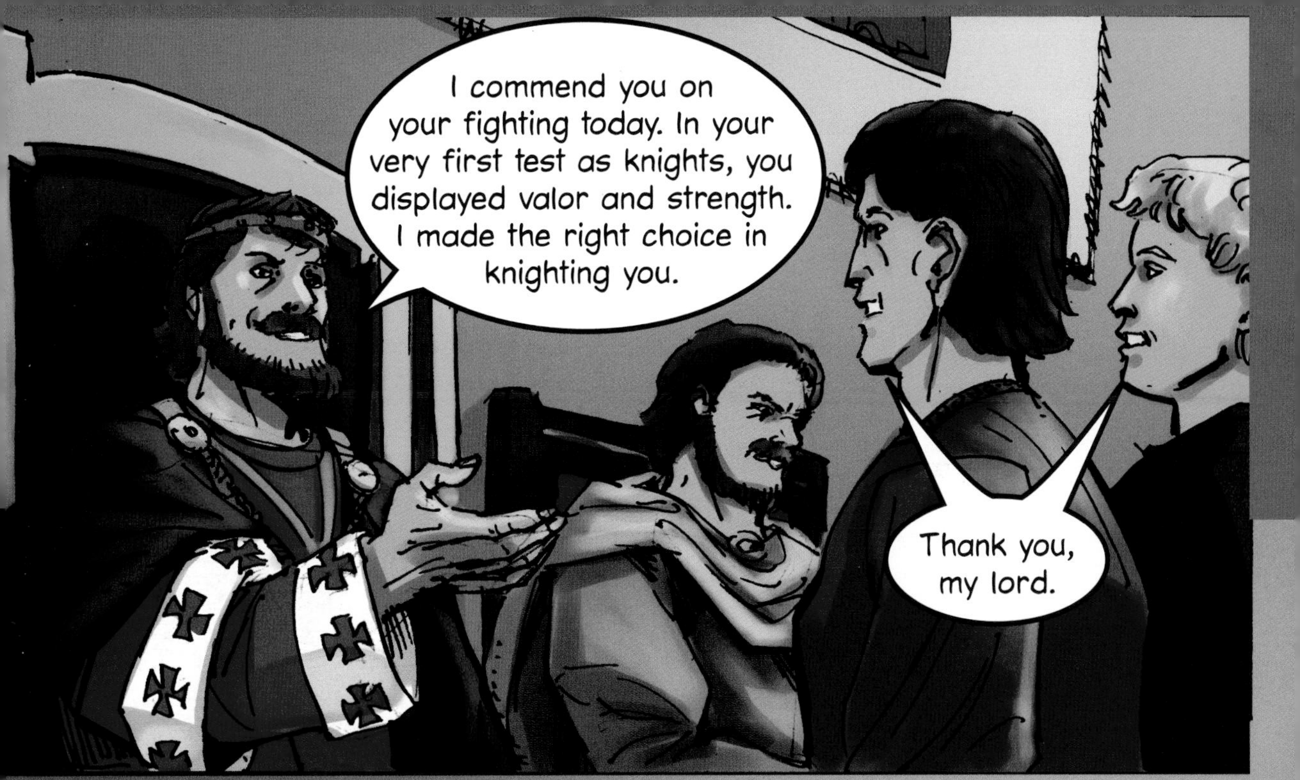
I commend you on your fighting today. In your very first test as knights, you displayed valor and strength. I made the right choice in knighting you.
Thank you, my lord.

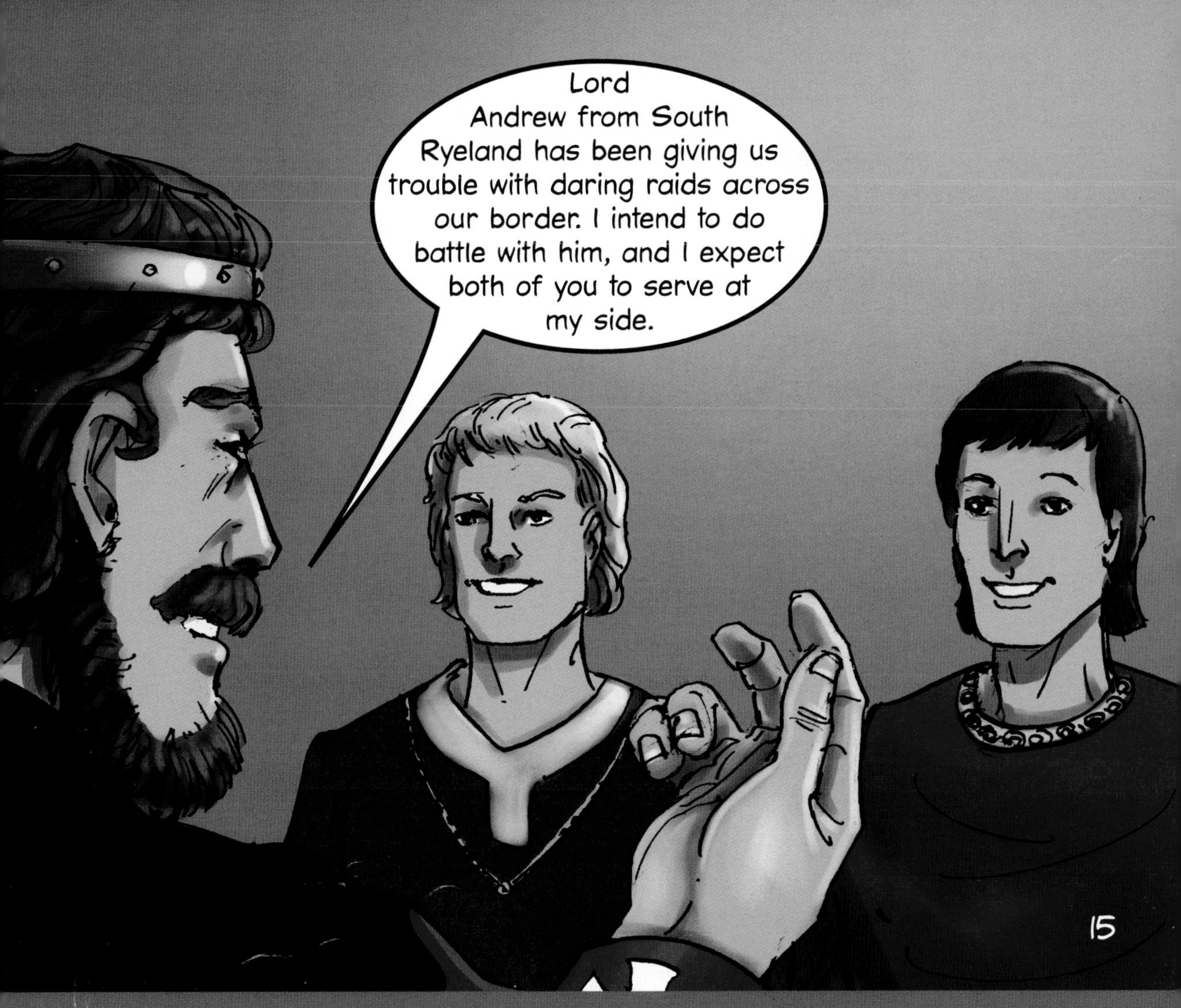
Lord Andrew from South Ryeland has been giving us trouble with daring raids across our border. I intend to do battle with him, and I expect both of you to serve at my side.

# TO ARMS!

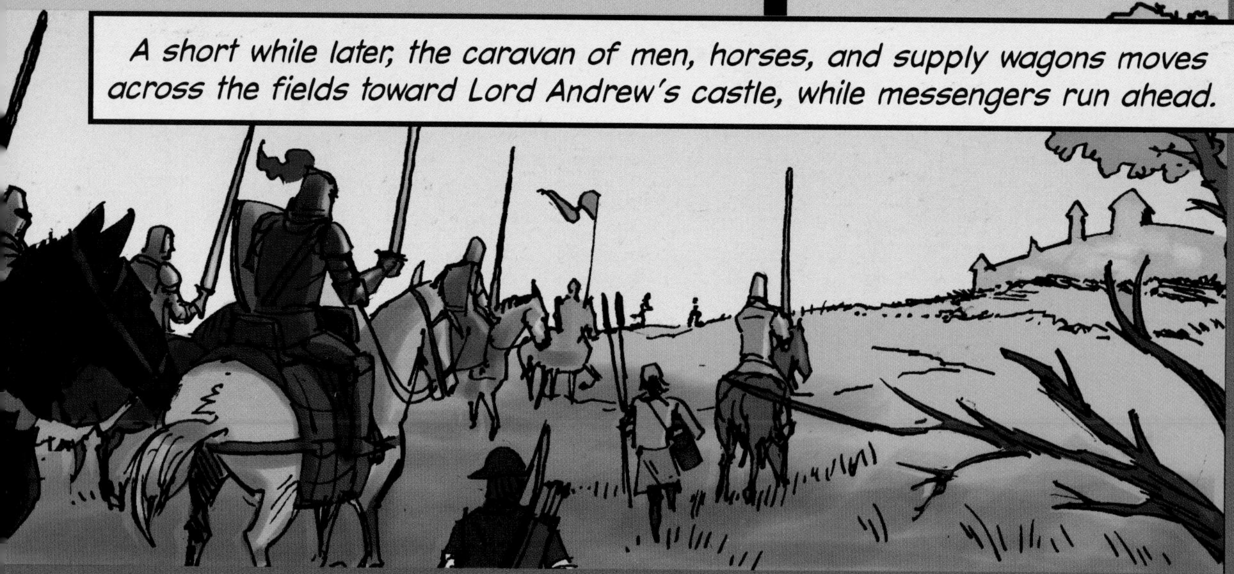
A short while later, the caravan of men, horses, and supply wagons moves across the fields toward Lord Andrew's castle, while messengers run ahead.

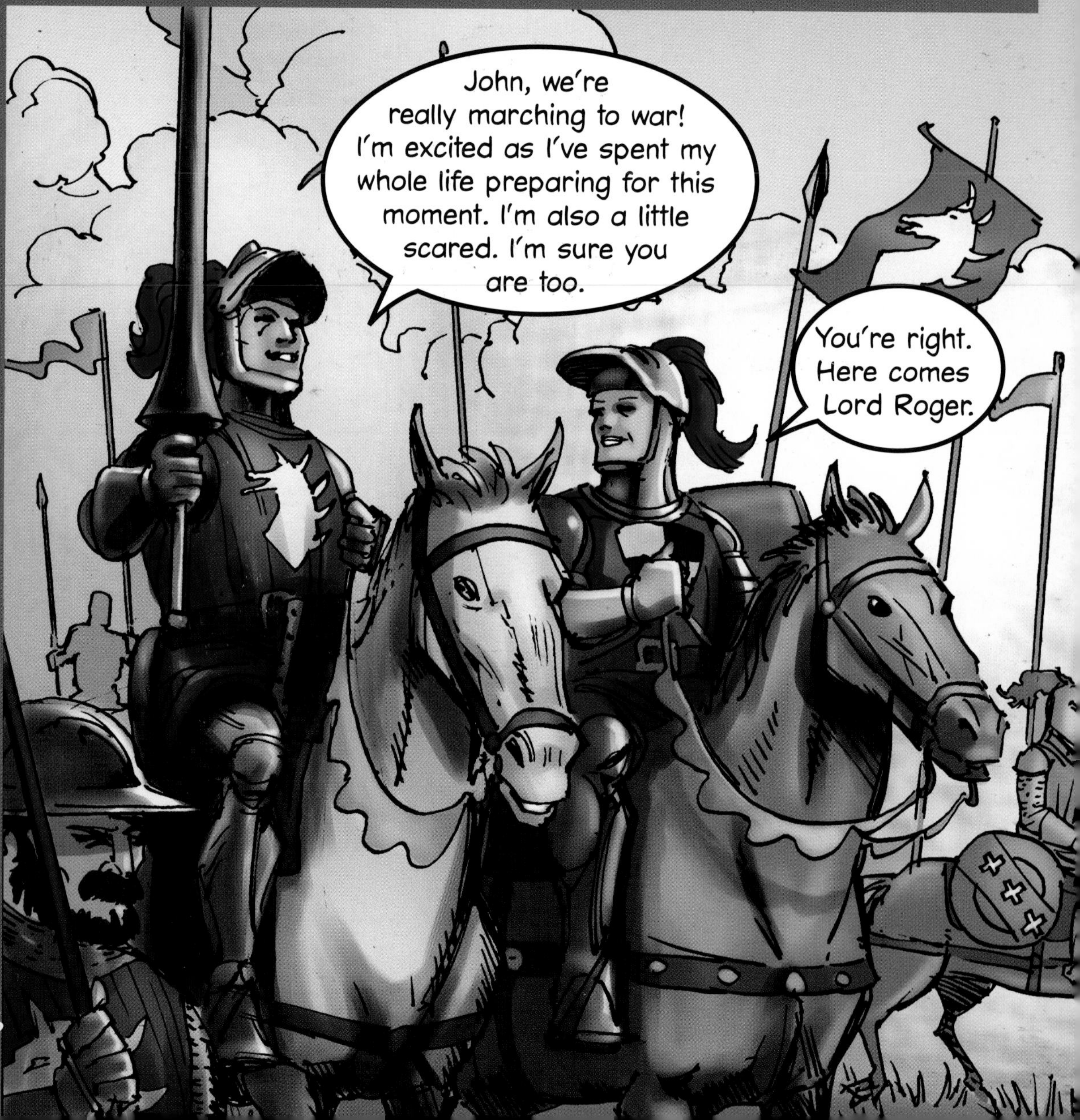
John, we're really marching to war! I'm excited as I've spent my whole life preparing for this moment. I'm also a little scared. I'm sure you are too.
You're right. Here comes Lord Roger.

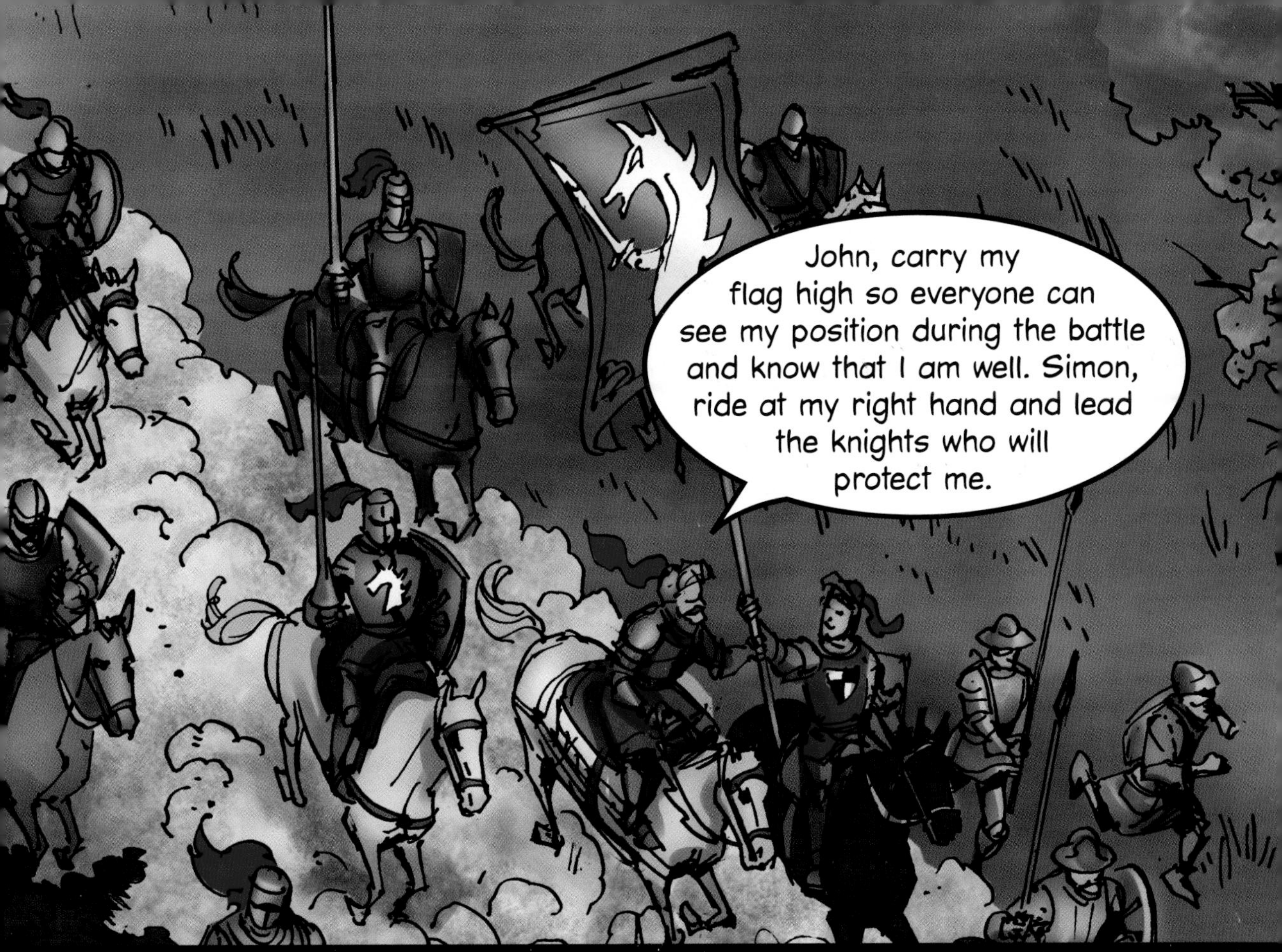
John, carry my flag high so everyone can see my position during the battle and know that I am well. Simon, ride at my right hand and lead the knights who will protect me.

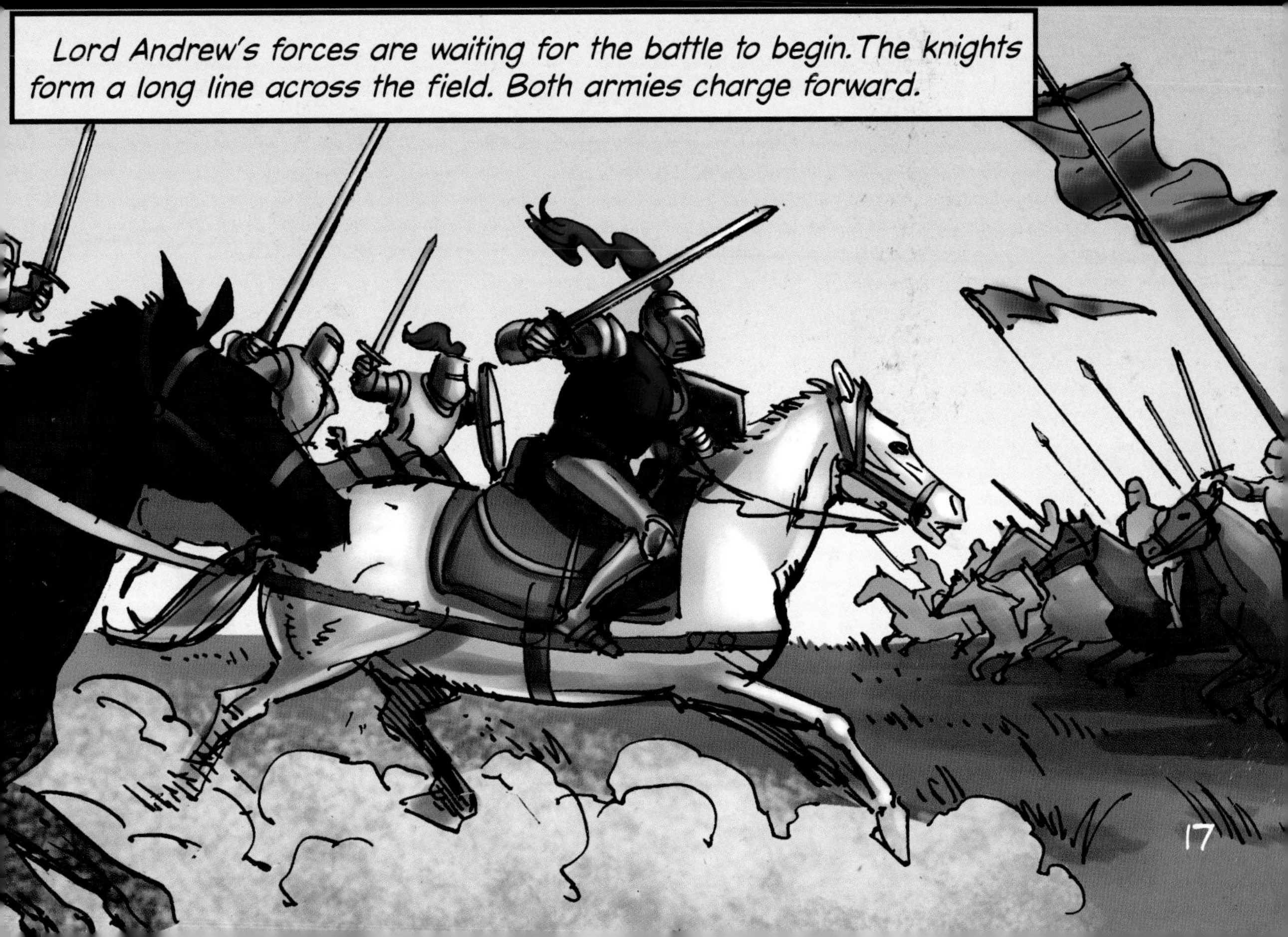
*Lord Andrew's forces are waiting for the battle to begin. The knights form a long line across the field. Both armies charge forward.*

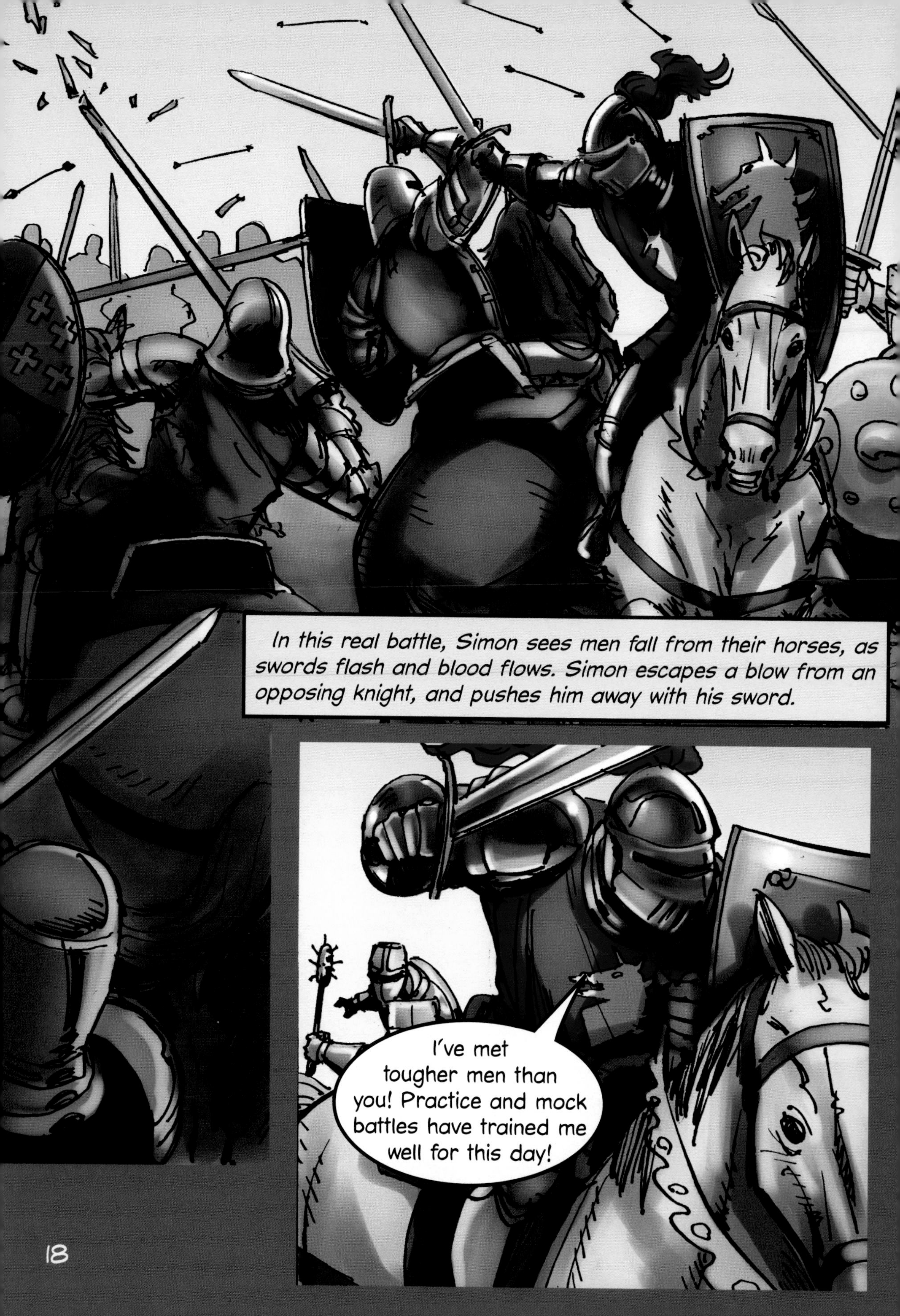
In this real battle, Simon sees men fall from their horses, as swords flash and blood flows. Simon escapes a blow from an opposing knight, and pushes him away with his sword.
I've met tougher men than you! Practice and mock battles have trained me well for this day!

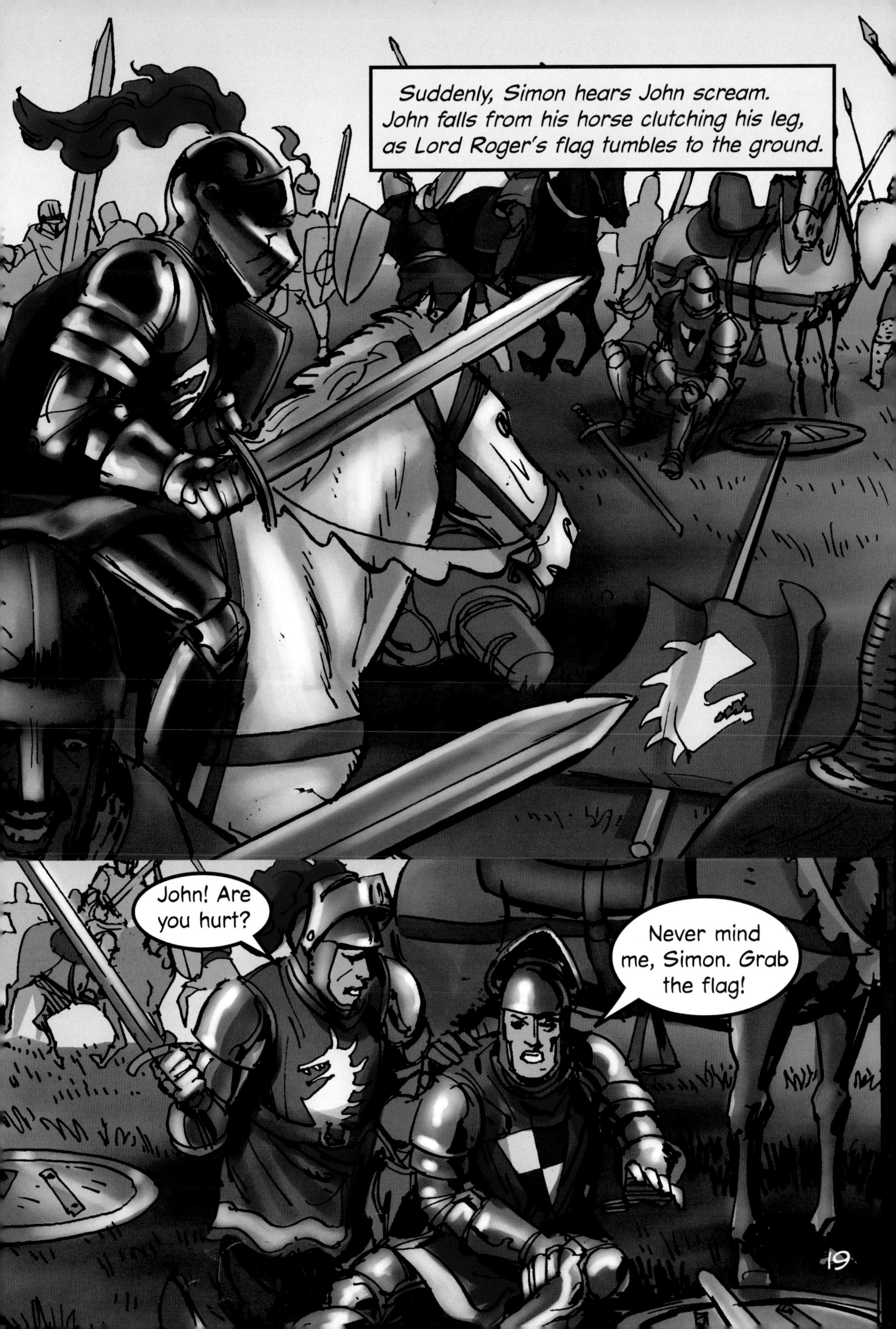
Suddenly, Simon hears John scream. John falls from his horse clutching his leg, as Lord Roger's flag tumbles to the ground.
John! Are you hurt?
Never mind me, Simon. Grab the flag!

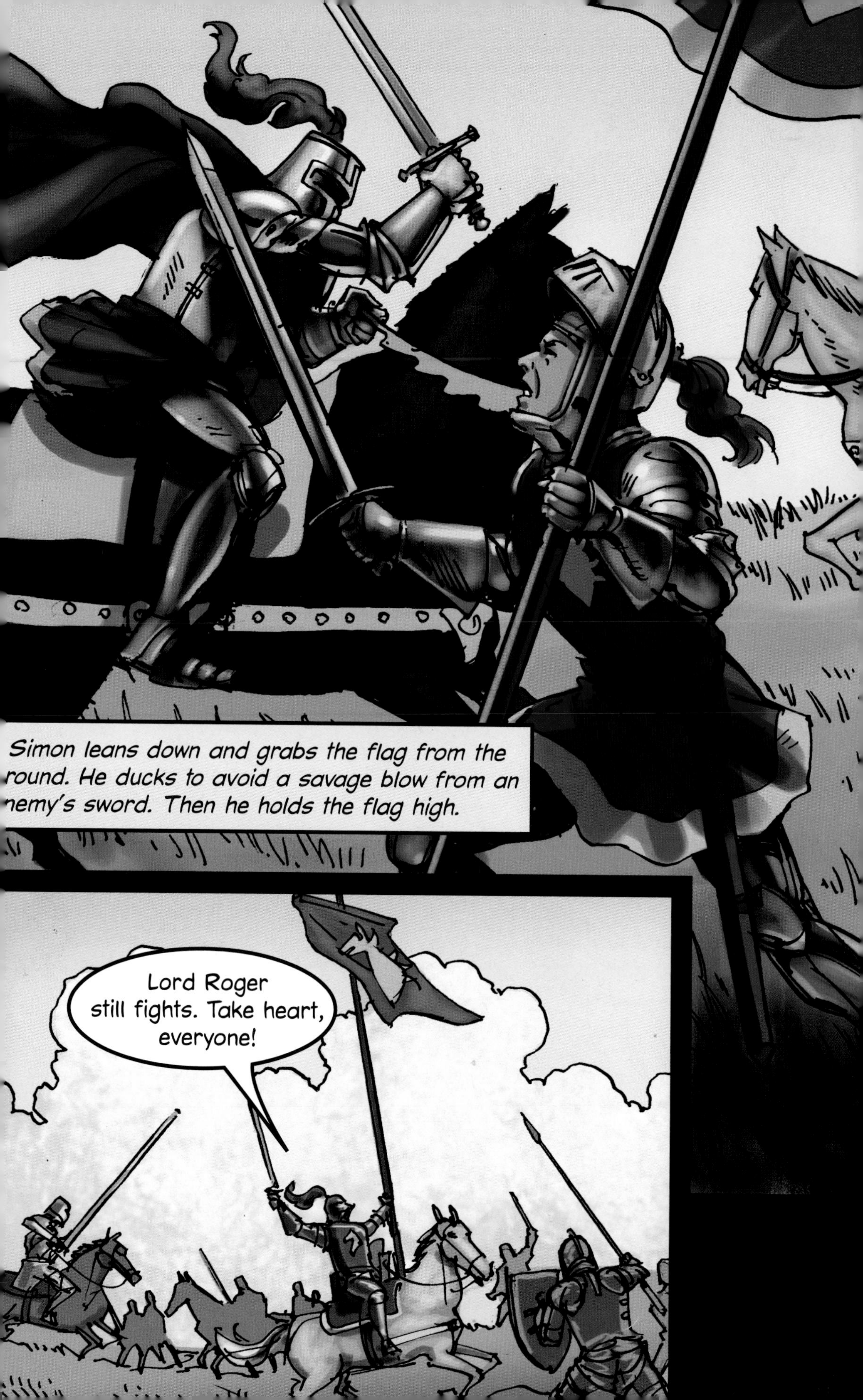
Simon leans down and grabs the flag from the round. He ducks to avoid a savage blow from an nemy's sword. Then he holds the flag high.
Lord Roger still fights. Take heart, everyone!

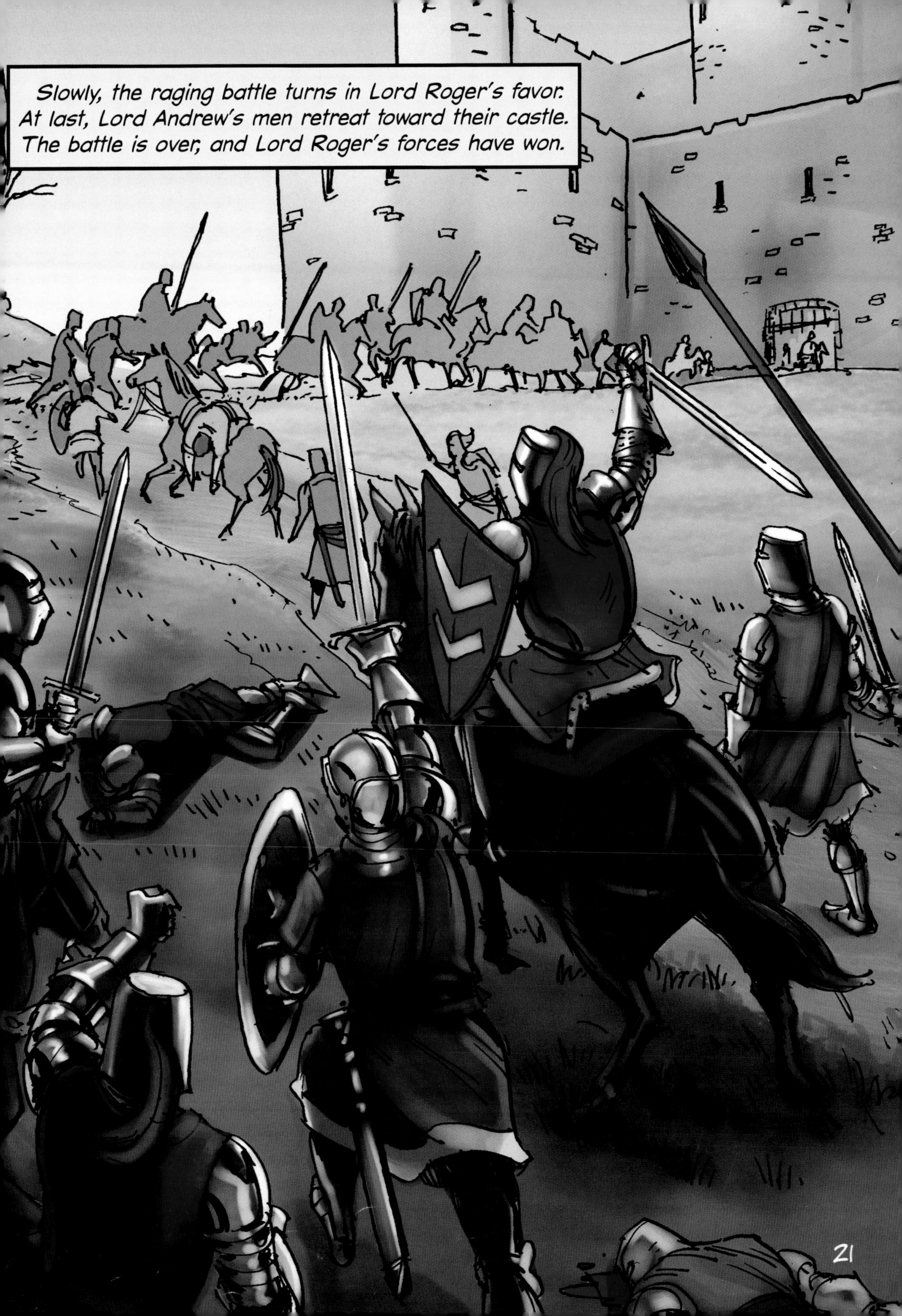
Slowly, the raging battle turns in Lord Roger's favor. At last, Lord Andrew's men retreat toward their castle. The battle is over, and Lord Roger's forces have won.

## AFTERMATH

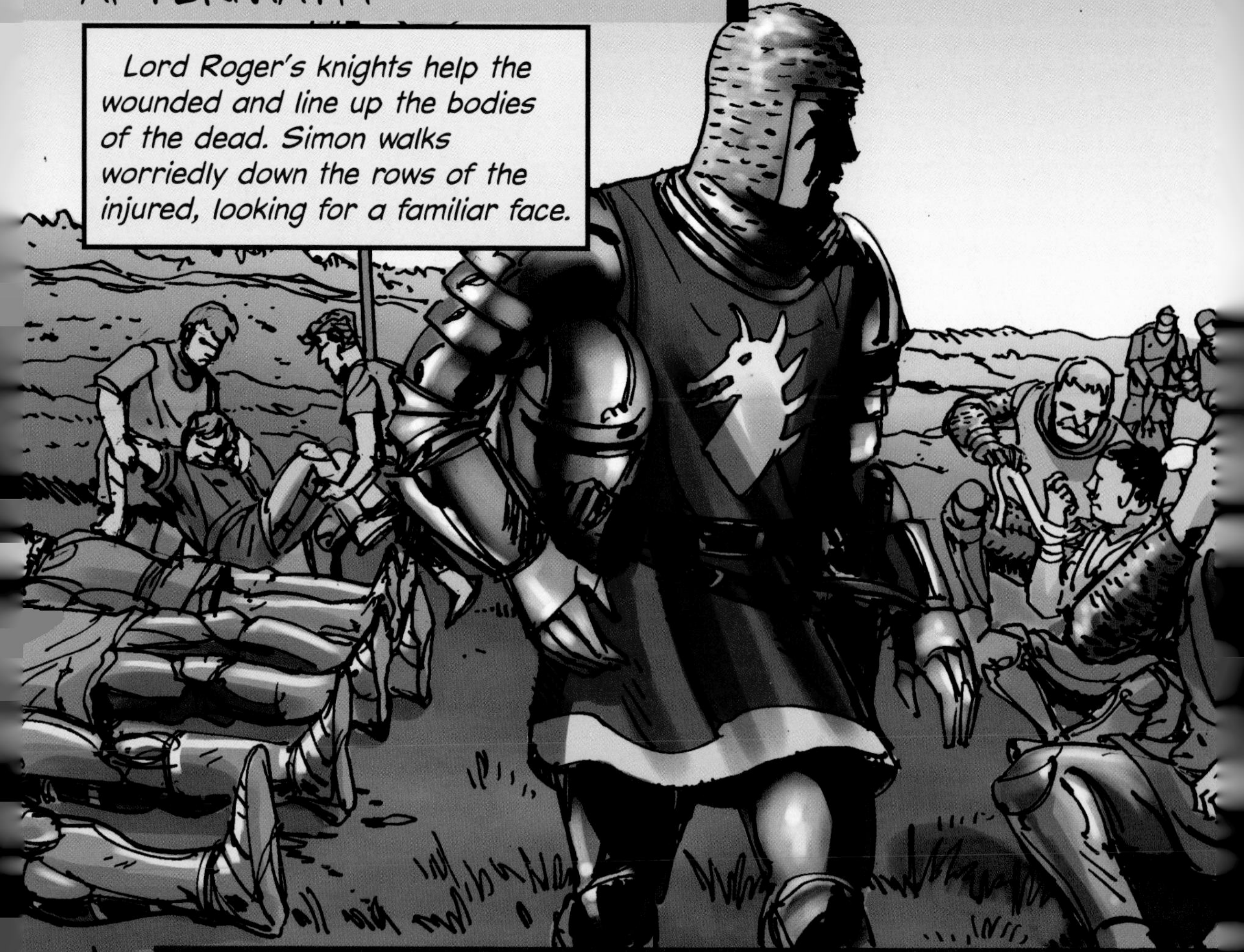
Lord Roger's knights help the wounded and line up the bodies of the dead. Simon walks worriedly down the rows of the injured, looking for a familiar face.

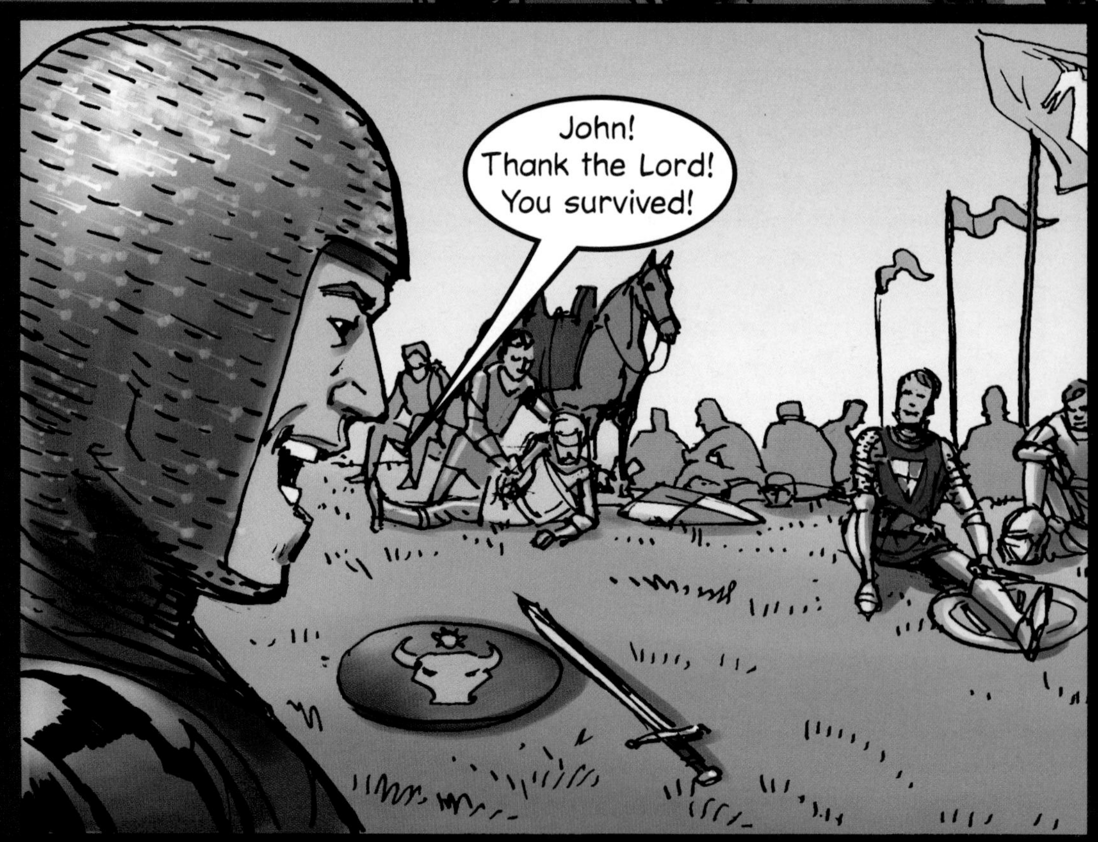
John! Thank the Lord! You survived!

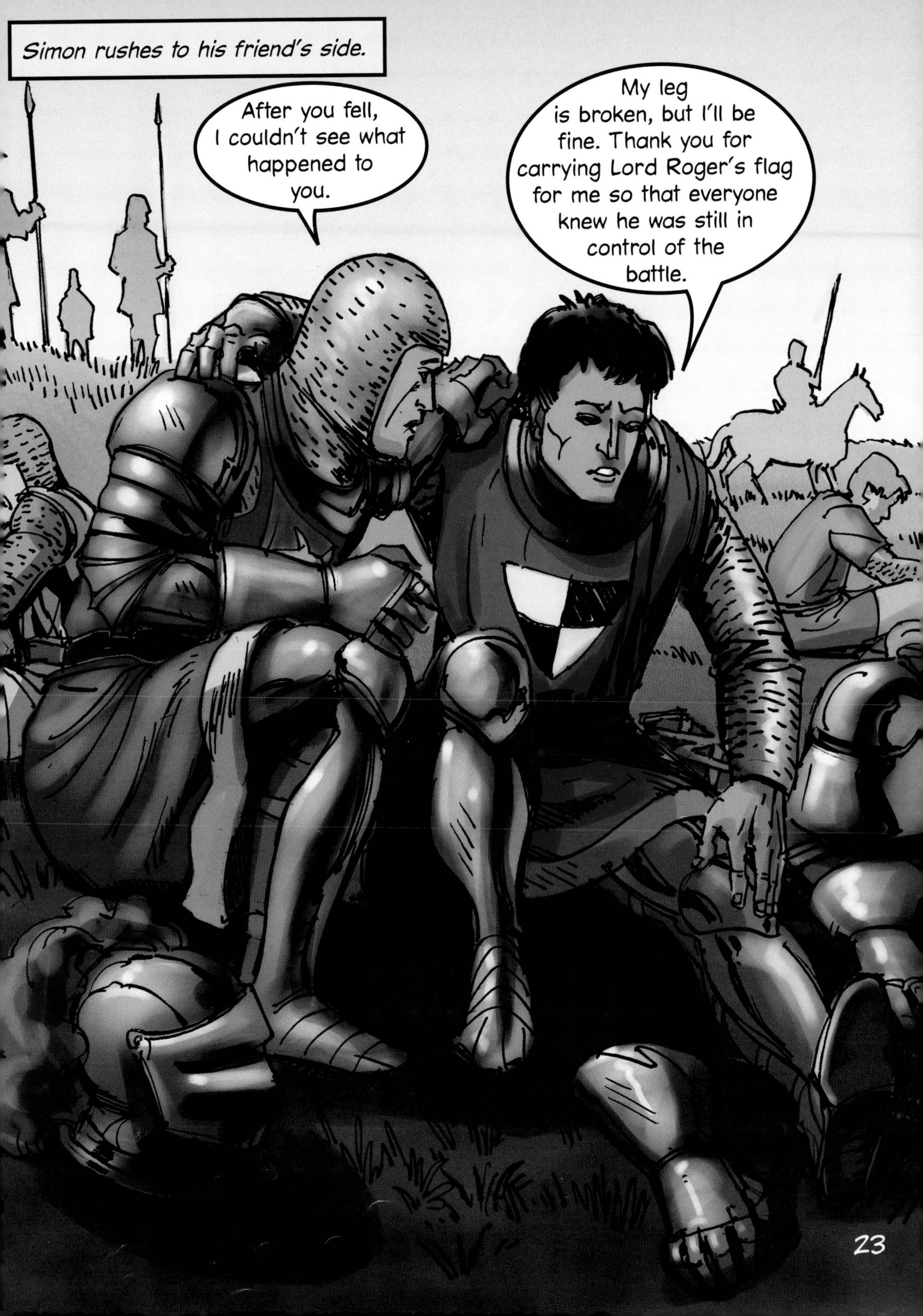
Simon rushes to his friend's side.
After you fell, I couldn't see what happened to you.
My leg is broken, but I'll be fine. Thank you for carrying Lord Roger's flag for me so that everyone knew he was still in control of the battle.

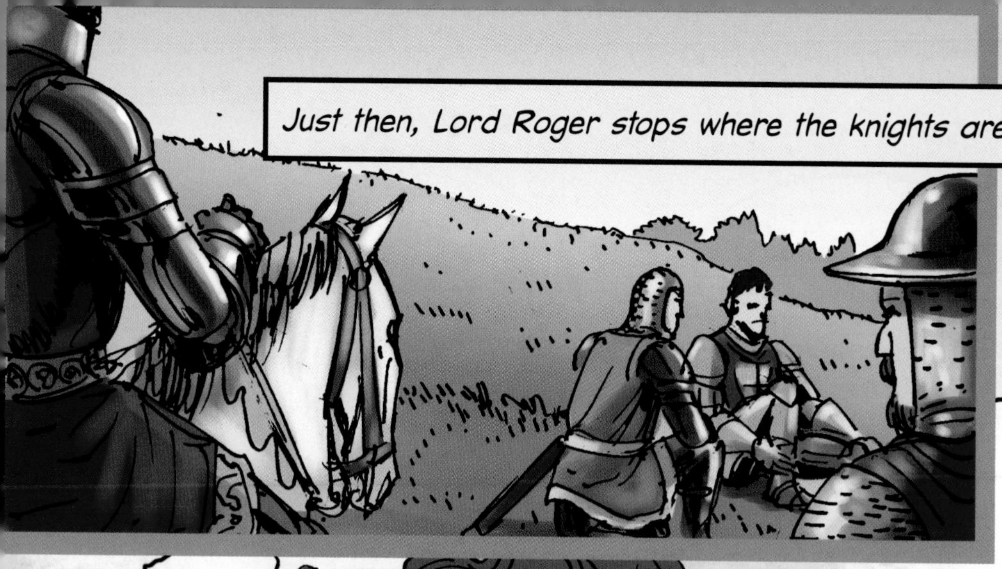
Just then, Lord Roger stops where the knights are sitting.

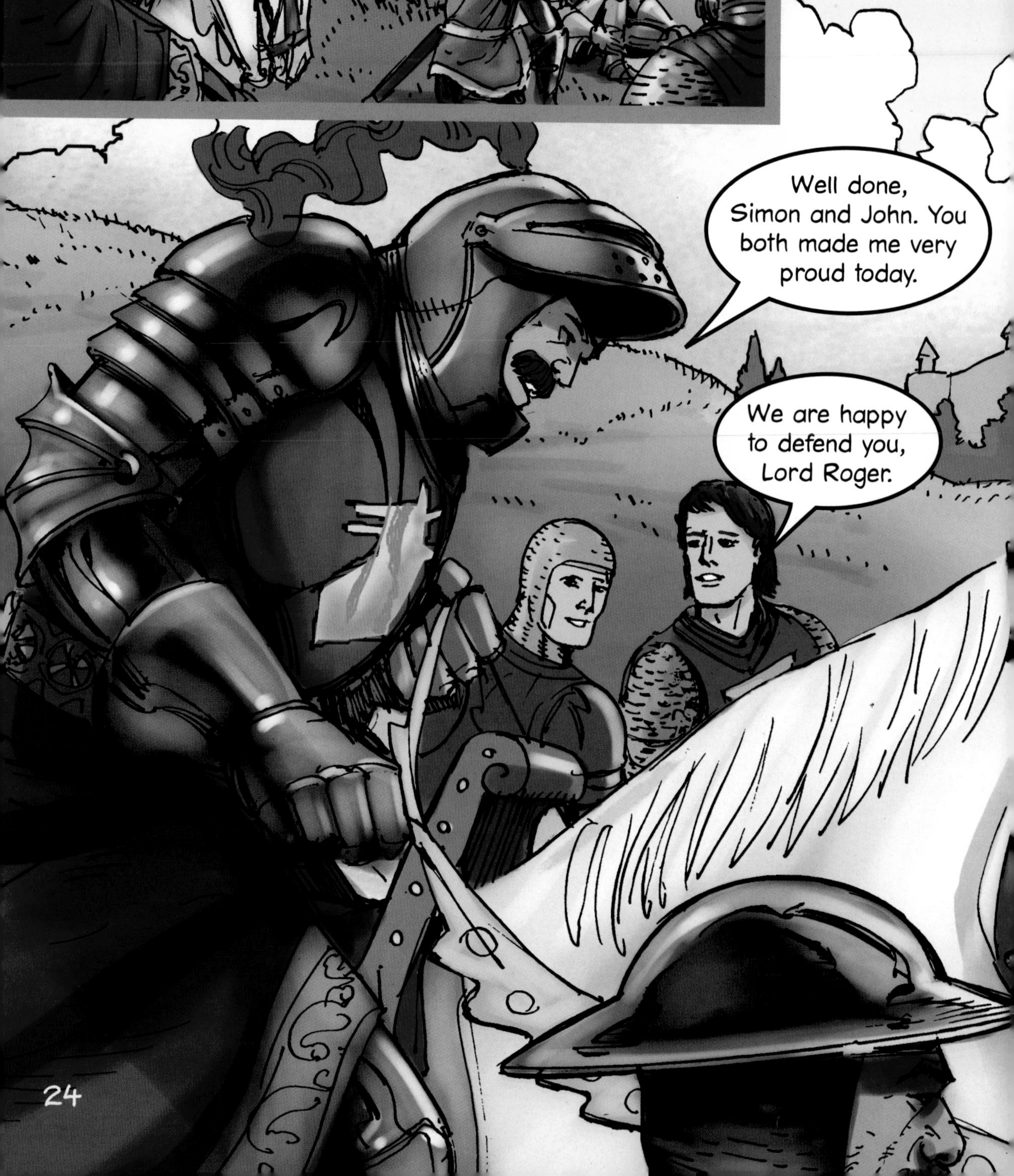
Well done, Simon and John. You both made me very proud today.
We are happy to defend you, Lord Roger.

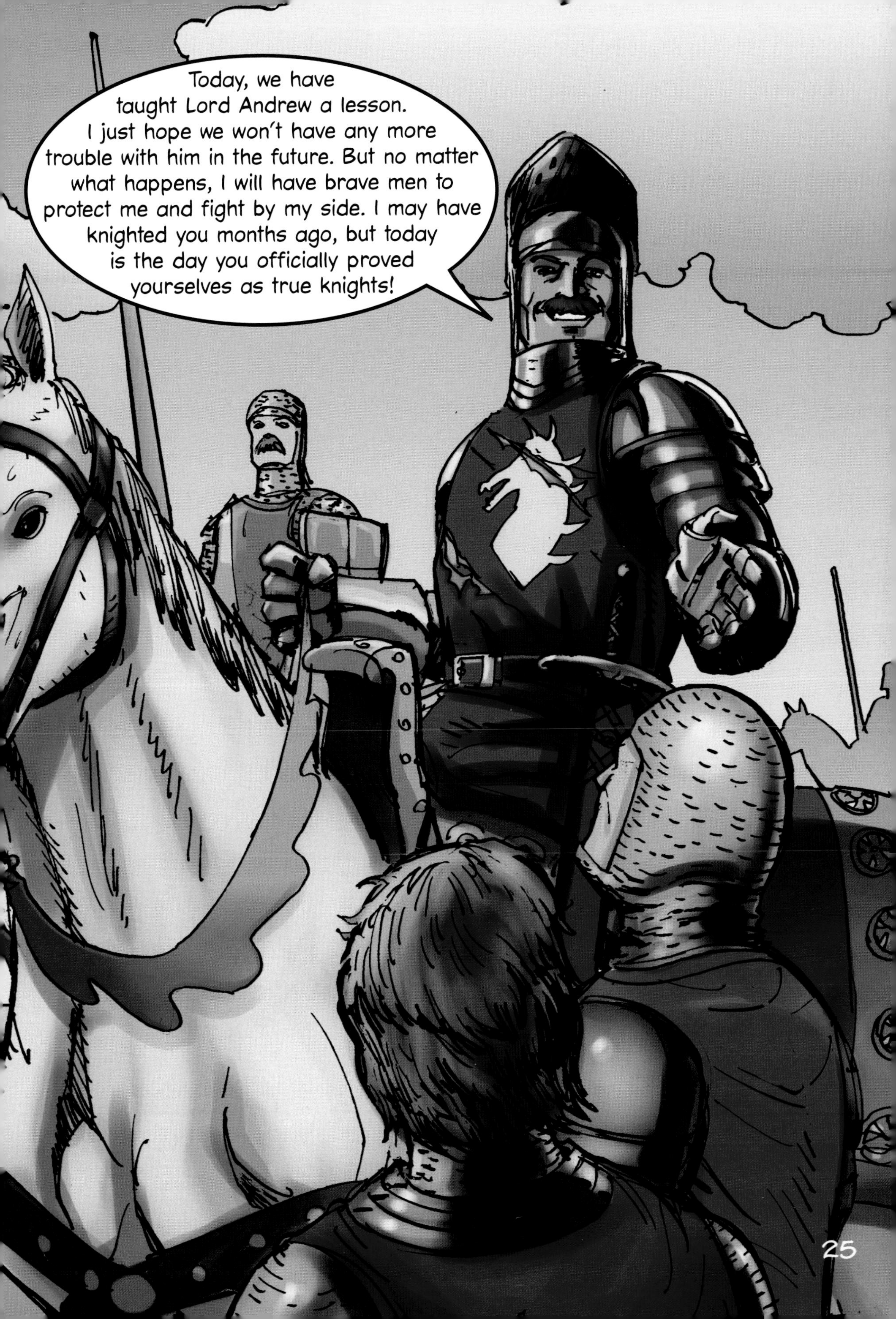
Today, we have taught Lord Andrew a lesson. I just hope we won't have any more trouble with him in the future. But no matter what happens, I will have brave men to protect me and fight by my side. I may have knighted you months ago, but today is the day you officially proved yourselves as true knights!

Between A.D. 800 and A.D. 1400, knights were the most important fighting force in Europe. At that time, Europe was divided into kingdoms, and each kingdom was further divided into lordships, or territories.

Each lord struggled to keep other lords from stealing his property and goods. Knights were used to make strong, loyal armies who offered protection against enemies. We often think of knights fighting in huge battles against other kingdoms, but in actuality, most battles were between smaller lordships.

*These knights are fighting in the Battle of Hastlings, which occured on October 14, 1066. Norman knights led by William the Conqueror defeated King Harold to take control of England.*

Not everyone could become a knight. A knight had to be born into the **noble** class. Usually, a knight's father was also a knight. Being a knight was expensive, because these fighters had to buy their own armor, weapons, and horses. They often had servants as well. Also, knights were viewed as heroes and were highly respected. Only men from the highest classes of society could become part of this honored group of fighters.

## Becoming a Knight

A knight's training began early. When he was about seven years old, a boy could become a **page**. He was sent away to a noble family, where he was taught how to behave, how to serve others, and how to ride a horse.

When the page was about fourteen, he became a squire. A squire was assigned to serve a knight. He was responsible for taking care of the knight's armor and weapons and helping him with everyday jobs. A squire could become a knight when he was 21 years old.

## Chivalry

Knights were supposed to live by a code called chivalry. Chivalry was a set of rules that told knights how to behave. Knights were supposed to be honorable and polite. They had to respect others and protect innocent people. Knights also had to be loyal to their lords and uphold the Christian religion.

## Tournaments

Lords held tournaments several times a year. Tournaments were festive events that entertained many people, but they also served a more serious purpose. As knights took part in mock battles and contests, they were putting their training to use and practicing what to do in a real battle.

*Today, many people enjoy acting out medieval battles. This man is dressed as a knight and is performing in a joust in Scotland.*

# A Knight in Shining Armor

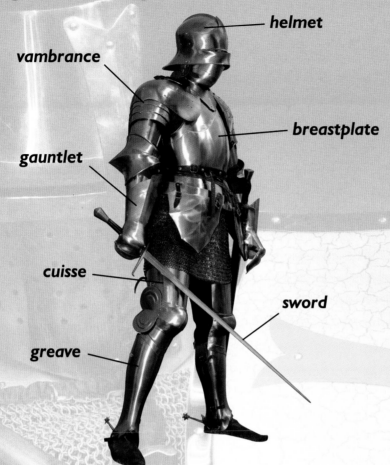

helmet

vambrance

breastplate

gauntlet

cuisse

sword

greave

# Websites

www.knight-medieval.com

www.knightsandarmor.com

www.kyrene.org/schools/brisas/sunda/ma/1jake.htm

www.mnsu.edu/emuseum/history/middleages/knighthood.html

history.howstuffworks.com/middle-ages/knight2.htm

library.thinkquest.org/10949/fief/medknight.html

# Glossary

**armor** (AR-mur): A metal covering worn by knights for protection.

**caravan** (KA-ruh-van): A group of people traveling together.

**chivalry** (SHIV-uhl-ree): Behavior that is polite and helpful.

**joust** (JOUST): A battle between two knights who are riding on horseback and carrying lances. Whoever is still sitting on his horse after the contest is the winner.

**lance** (LANSS): A long spear used by knights who are jousting while on horseback.

**mock** (MOK): To pretend or imitate. A mock battle is a fake or pretend battle.

**noble** (NOH-buhl): A person of high rank or birth.

**page** (PAYJ): A young boy who is training to become a knight. Training usually begins at around age 7.

**squire** (SKWIRE): A young man who helps a knight. The squire usually becomes a knight after years of service.

**tournament** (TUR-nuh-muhnt): An event or contest. Knights had jousting tournaments as a way to practice for real battles.

**valor** (VAL-ur): Great bravery or courage.

# Index



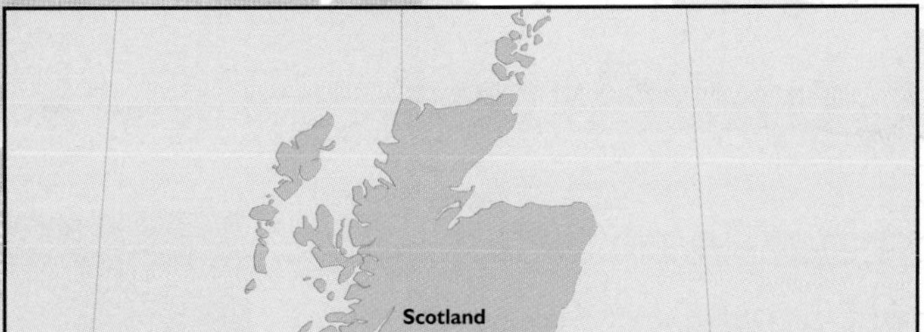
Scotland
North Sea
Isle of Man
Irish Sea
Ireland
England
Wales
St George's Channel
Bristol Channel
Strait of Dover
France
English Channel

*Some of the greatest battles fought among knights occurred throughout England and other European countries.*

## About the Author

Joanne Mattern is the author of more than 300 books for children. She has written about a variety of subjects, including sports, history, biography, animals, and science. She loves bringing nonfiction subjects to life for children! Joanne lives in New York State with her husband, four children, and assorted pets.

## About the Artist

Chris Marrinan is an artist who has created images for many things, including everything from billboards to video game covers! He got his start in the comic book business drawing for the comic book publishers DC Comics, Marvel, Dark Horse, and Image. Chris has drawn many comic icons, such as Wonder Woman, Spider-Man, and Wolverine. He lives in Northern California with his two children.